The Circle of Kourabies

A century-old tale of honey, coffee, salt, lemon, paper, whiskey, and cigarettes.

By Kathy Crane
and Sandia Harrison

The Circle of Kourabies

A century-old tale of honey, coffee, salt, lemon, paper, whiskey, and cigarettes.

HISTORICAL NOTE

This book is based on true events and reflects the culmination of extensive research using family archives, immigration records, and period sources. Every effort has been made to portray historical details accurately. However, many records from this era were handwritten and incomplete, and the documentation standards of the early twentieth century differ from those of today's digital age. Certain interpretations and reconstructed details have been included to fill unavoidable gaps in the historical record.

RECIPE DISCLAIMER

The recipes in this book have been transcribed from verbal instruction to the best abilities of the authors. Although they have been tested, absolute accuracy cannot be guaranteed. Ingredients and cooking styles vary widely by region. We honor and respect the differences of every cook.

Published by ECS, Fallbrook, California

Cover design and interior layout by
Sandia Harrison

ISBN: 979-8-9987737-7-8

First Edition

For permissions or inquiries, please contact:
ECS Publishing, Inc. Fallbrook, California

The real inheritance of a family is not gold or land,
but the unseen energy of memory carried forward.

CONTENTS

THE TELLING (ΤΟ ΔΙΗΓΗΜΑ) | STORY

THE TABLE (TO TPAΠEZI) | RECIPIES

THE AFTERWORD (ΤΟ ΕΠΙΜΕΤΡΟ) | NOTES

DEDICATION

By Kathy Crane

This book is dedicated to my daughters and grandchildren. Thank you all for being such a special part of my life. May this story bring happiness to everyone in the kitchen and out. Thanks especially to Penelope, the greatest mother-in-law ever, who taught me how to cook many of the dishes that appear in this book.

THE CIRCLE OF KOURABIES

Ο ΚΥΚΛΟΣ ΤΩΝ ΚΟΥΡΑΜΠΙΕΔΩΝ

CHAPTER ONE

The Candymaker

As a young girl, Penelope didn't like to cook. She only liked to eat.

1898. KORONI, GREECE

She could usually be found on the *tarátsa* while her grandmother was cooking. After she came home from school and finished her homework and chores, she'd sit in an ancient wooden chair, swinging her tiny legs and picking at the peeling aqua paint. From that vantage point, she could watch the villagers below while enjoying the rich aromas coming from the primitive kitchen inside.

It was a humble villa, although she didn't realize it at the time. Even from three stories up, she could not see the nearby harbor dotted with caiques, their patched sails leaning into the wind, nor the nets hung from the rigging to dry, fluttering like tattered flags. But the smell of fresh sea air was always present. Gulls flew by, loudly calling out to one another mid-air.

As she grew, Penelope spent less time on the rooftop. She no longer had hours to waste on mere daydreams. If the patio was already swept and the plants didn't need water, there was only one time she could reliably be found there: *trápeza* night.

Once a week, her father hosted the same circle of men for cards. By nightfall, the small dining area thickened into a haze of cigarette smoke, steeped in coffee and lively arguments over politics and the season's olive yields.

The sound of dog-eared cards slapping against a table was as much a part of village life as the church bell. It wasn't game night she minded, but the company. Most of her father's friends were harmless. The Vrachonis brothers were not.

She estimated they must be at least as old as her father, yet both spoke to her as if she were their schoolmate. Penelope, on the other hand, was expected to address them with respect.

If she happened to be downstairs when they arrived, they would go out of their way to greet her, standing too close, fingers brushing her hair as they leaned in to speak, their breath sour with smoke.

Once seated with the men, she would overhear them boasting about how they had "fought the Turks in '97," though all of Koroni knew they had really spent the war far from danger, guarding a supply route near Kalamata. When pensions were later offered to wounded veterans, each wrapped an arm and claimed to have been injured "on the front lines."

Neither had faced real combat, but forged paperwork was enough to grant them modest stipends, funds they treated as proof of their supposed superiority. Both bought ornate iron gates for their perfectly ordinary homes. After that, nobody in the village ever glimpsed the inside of either house, though the brothers were quick to insist they had all the modern conveniences.

If Penelope's father bought her mother a new stock pot, they had a better one. If he refinished their kitchen table, theirs was larger and made of finer wood.

One of their wives did laundry for wealthier families; the other sold her home-baked bread at the agora. While the two women worked hard and raised the children, the Vrachonis brothers lounged at home, smoking and complaining that "Greece doesn't do enough to honor its heroes."

Penelope carried herself with a kind of warmth that drew people in. She had a wide smile, soft eyes, and a face of graceful heart shape that she would tilt to one side when she listened to people talk. She had wavy, mahogany-colored hair. She had never liked trousers. Even her nightgowns were just that – gowns. She wore only dresses in the daytime, usually floral.

She lived with her parents, grandparents and siblings.

She already knew the rhythm of work. In their world, everything required motion. Water had to be brought and bread kneaded. Penelope would help bring bushels of clothing to stone wash platforms on the village's end to be scrubbed clean, then carried home wet and even heavier. Once she completed her schooling, morning light didn't signal rest from the day before, only another round of the same. Floors were swept, then swept again before dusk. Her mother and grandmother moved through the kitchen as if time itself demanded obedience, their hands forever busy.

In spite of it all, laughter came easily to Penelope. Hers was a refreshing demeanor in a town where economic hardship left many somber day after day.

Still, the only time Penelope used hot coals was to heat the steel iron to press the linens and her father's shirts. Everyone knew a good wife would need to know how to cook.

It bothered her.

In Koroni, at that time, a girl nearing marriage without cooking skills would have been seen as a source of shame and gossip, both for herself and her parents. It suggested she was "not ready to be a wife," which was one of the harshest judgments someone her age could face.

It was complicated. It wasn't that the two women lacked the patience to allow her to try. She knew they would never deliberately humiliate her either.

Well, that is, unless she did something clumsy like kick the wash bucket over for the umpteenth time.

They meant well, but they also couldn't allow mistakes in the kitchen. Their reputation rode on meals not only coming out correctly, but also timely. Through her growing years, it had always seemed like there was never time to slow down enough to allow her to learn.

But Penelope didn't look at it that way. She blamed only herself.

Her mother knew, and felt guilty. Her father stood helpless in the face of it. Over the years he had asked his wife and mother-in-law countless times to allow his daughter to spend more time making meals. At first, he did so, patiently. When nothing came of it, he became sterner. He told them that they really needed to teach Penelope how to cook.

Both women always assured him that they would. It is likely that they meant it in that moment. But when Penelope couldn't slice potatoes or pick basil off the stems as quickly as they could, they believed they were being loving when they simply took over.

So it would remain a secret, as Penelope approached the age of marriage: she didn't know how to cook at all.

Late spring, 1909, brought good news. Her father had found a suitor. He was a fine young man, from a background wealthier than their own. In Koroni, at that time, that meant something. Most of the villagers had very little. Also, he told her, their two families had always gotten along well.

The news spread quickly in the horio (the village) of the upcoming nuptials. It would be a peaceful union. He, an earnest and hardworking guy, and she, a charming woman nearly impossible to dislike. A fitting union. Until...

She took one look at him and decided: absolutely not.

The shock rippled through Koroni like someone had suggested canceling Easter.

"Unheard of," the newlywed wives Penelope's age in the village whispered to one other as they carried baskets of potatoes and garlic from the outdoor market. Many of them had been her classmates.

«Τσού, τσού, τσού,»

"tsk, tsk, tsk," the grandmothers clicked their tongues as they gathered in the courtyard after church.

"Can't understand it," the men were overheard saying to the local merchant and barber, shaking their heads.

Privately, Penelope bore the weight of her family's disappointment. Her parents didn't dare raise their voices. Few had glass windowpanes. They were afraid the shuttered windows wouldn't keep out their words of dissatisfaction with their daughter.

She was too afraid to tell them what she saw that they didn't. He had always acted like a richer man than he was. At school, she had seen his shoes; full of holes. He had no others. The shoes he wore to meet her that day were in terrible shape. The fine clothing he wore was ill-fitting. She was certain it had all been borrowed.

That boy was a fake. Everyone in school had known it.

He was the son of one of her father's friends, one of the Vrachonis brothers. There was no way they could force her to marry him. They could whip her until she was black and blue, and she still wouldn't do it.

But another truth still loomed large; her lack of cooking skills. Nobody was in the mood for a second wave of embarrassment. And if that lapse in her domestic training was discovered after a cancelled wedding, then spread around the village, it would be just that.

Penelope's father was a popular man around town. The Vrachonis brothers had not taken the rejection well.

In the days that followed, Penelope had noticed that she was no longer seeing her friends around town. Once, as she walked out of the grain and milling store, her cheerful whistles came to an abrupt stop as she detected the sound of sandals scuffling on stone. Had someone hurried away when they saw her? Were they avoiding her? What could those awful people be saying?

Her father knew that the only way to quiet things down, and probably the one way he could save face personally, was to end it all by finding another suitor. Quickly. Someone who wouldn't announce from the top of the nearby hills that his new wife could clean, but not even boil an egg.

He began quietly asking among only those he truly trusted. Discretion was everything now; another misstep would only confirm the whispers.

That was when he discovered what had been hidden in plain sight. One of his closest friends confided that his son had been admiring Penelope from a distance for years. They had grown up in similar circles, shared the same festivals and feasts. The boy's family were confectioners. He would give Penelope small treats from time to time when they were children. The two got along well enough, but were never close enough for anyone to suspect romance, or to imagine them as a couple.

1909. CONFECTIONERS FROM MESSENE

The truth? Young Louis was kind of half-invisible. The good part: he was not the kind of figure who inspired village gossip, nor had anyone ever heard him say a negative thing. He simply blended in. He wasn't handsome, but he wasn't bad-looking either. Just a regular-looking gent. Short, a little round in the middle, the type who seemed winded after climbing the harbor steps. Shy, too, painfully so. He never said much.

And yet, behind the shyness, there it was: the quietest crush in Koroni. Nobody, even his closest friends, ever knew.

Back at home, Penelope reacted with utter shock. She asked her father incredulously "You're not talking about that candymaker boy who blushes if someone so much as asks him the time, are you?"

Her mouth began to form the letter "n," as in "NO."

Her father interrupted.

"Yes, that's him, and he plans to move to America.

Silence. Heaviness in the room.

America.

Penelope looked at her father, who was staring her straight in the eyes.

After a long pause, her father never breaking his gaze, "okay," she practically whispered.

America. Even the word carried a kind of promise. Everyone said so. People were leaving their villages and moving there by the shipfuls.

And for Penelope, it meant even more than just a faraway country. It meant places where no one knew her secrets, somewhere where her refusal of one suitor would not echo for years, and where a woman might step a little beyond the narrow roles her village had already laid out for her. The very thought of it said "freedom."

She imagined wide avenues instead of dusty paths, homes with glass in the windows, shiny motorcars, and markets overflowing with vegetables and produce she had never seen. Most of all, it meant possibility. Life in her village was all she had ever known, but she could feel herself already outgrowing it. America was vast, untold, waiting. All of her friends said so. She could hardly wait to tell them.

As for the candymaker's kid Louis, well, he came to the house with his father and mother, his uncle and his grandfather. The entire clan got there faster than you could roll out a batch of diples. After an evening of strong coffee and high speed and higher volume conversation, the marriage was arranged. Everyone was relieved, even Penelope. She told herself she'd get to know him later, in the small, ordinary days they would share. He seemed a gentle fellow; how bad could it be?

At the time, Louis could no more roast a lamb than patch a sail, but he could temper sugar with patience. After all, he had spent his life surrounded by expert candy makers. He understood instinctively how to coax sweet things into balance. It was a skill that would serve them both well. He would help his new wife learn to cook with a smile. Never causing her the slightest shame or embarrassment.

Penelope, for her part, spent those last months in Koroni hardly ever leaving her mother's and grandmother's sides in their small kitchen. She watched and repeated their actions until her hands could follow theirs without thinking. Every ancient recipe was absorbed with the finality of someone who knew her future depended on it. She measured by sight, judged heat by feel, memorized the timing of a recipe not by minutes but by the look of a sauce or the scent of herbs in the pan. With her wedding approaching, the work reshaped her. The carefree girl now shared space inside with a young woman who understood what lay ahead.

When the day finally came for her to leave, she would board the ship carrying no written notes. The knowledge lived in her hands and senses, a gift from loved ones she might never see again. One they had given her to open in a land far away, a new world.

She was fifteen.

SIDERITIS HERBAL INFUSION
GREEK MOUNTAIN TEA

INGREDIENTS

- 2–3 dried stalks of sideritis (ironwort, Greek mountain tea), including blossoms.

- 2 cups water

- Honey (optional, to taste)

- Lemon slice (optional, to serve)

HOW TO MAKE IT

1. Rinse the dried stalks quickly to remove any dust.

2. Bring 2 cups of water to a gentle boil in a small pot.

3. Add the sideritis stalks and reduce heat to a simmer. Cover and let steep for 5–7 minutes, until the water turns golden and fragrant.

4. Strain into cups. Sweeten with honey if desired, and serve with a slice of lemon on the side.

In 1910, herbal infusions ("τσάι του βουνού" tsai tou vounou, literally "mountain tea") would have been common, and very different from British-style tea drinking. They were rustic, homemade, and tied to the land.

Servings: 2
Prep Time: 5 minutes
Cook/Steep Time: 7 minutes
Total Time: 12 minutes
Adaptations/Notes: Page 167

1909. ELLIS ISLAND, NEW YORK

Louis traveled ahead. He arrived in New York in the spring. The immigration officer looked up at him like he was another piece of cargo coming down the ramp.

"Name," he scowled.

He gave him his name, Elias Haralambakis.

The man grumbled something like, "I heard "Louis Harrison.""

So that is what he wrote down.

With legal documents in a clenched hand, and a new moniker, the unbiddenly-minted Mr. Harrison made his way to East Saint Louis, where he had a small network of other Greeks waiting for him. A city that shared his name. That felt regal, in a sense. His America felt like opportunity for work and dignity after a childhood full of suppressed dreams. Once he settled and found a place to live, he opened a candy store with his savings. Then, he sent for his new wife.

Penelope was scheduled to sail on January 3, 1910. Her ticket had been purchased and her trunk had been packed. But when the ship prepared to embark, she was not among the passengers. She had come down with a severe, unknown illness. No one could say what it was or how long it might last.

In New York, Louis waited at the port for hours, watching the gangway. Each cluster of travelers walking down the ramp gave him hope, while each passing minute stripped it away. By late afternoon, there was nobody left to disembark. The ship pulled away from the dock, slowly moving outward into the harbor to anchor for the night. He kept watching even then, although he was already certain she was not there.

1909. KORONI, GREECE

Days earlier, Penelope remembered regaining consciousness. She didn't know where she was. This was not her bedroom. She closed her eyes, too weak to keep them open, as she tried to listen. Her mother's voice, a teakettle. Someone else was there, another lady who sounded familiar but she wasn't able to place her.

Through her closed eyes, she saw movement cause light to flicker in the room, so she opened them just a little.

«Κούκλα μου! Παναγία μου, σε ευχαριστώ!»

"My doll! My Holy Virgin Mary, thank you!"

Her mother's throat was rigid with emotion when she saw her daughter's half-open eyes. Penelope wanted to speak. She had so many questions. Her mother's hand was still slightly damp from wringing out freshly washed towels. When she clasped her daughter's, still hot and feverish, her cool hand was so soothing that Penelope couldn't help but fall back to sleep.

She drifted in and out of consciousness for days on end, fighting unsuccessfully to remain fully awake. During moments of lucidity, she caught whispers of the shame of a canceled sailing, though she didn't really know what it meant.

Until one late morning when she woke up stirring and restless. She had been dreaming about a man standing in the middle of an oil refinery. Smoke was billowing out everywhere and pilot flames were lit here and there. The sooty sky looked dark as night.

Louis.

"Mamá!" She shrieked.

The manifest from the S.S. Athinai, dated January 3, 1910, noting that Penelope had been "discharged" from the voyage. Her entry is on line number 23.

Moments later, an elderly woman rushed to the open doorway.

"She's just gone out for a few minutes, blessed girl, but thank the lord you are speaking," she said with a radiant smile.

Penelope recognized her now. Mrs. Pappas.

Of course. Years ago, before she retired, Mrs. Pappas had been a nurse at the hospital in Kalamata. Penelope's parents wouldn't have been able to afford treatment there, and it was unlikely she would have survived the journey anyway. She had never been there, but she had heard it was "half a day by cart, more if the rain's bad. Three hours by horse, if the road holds."

Mrs. Pappas, who lived alone, just steps away from their house, had taken Penelope in to try to nurse her back to health. Her father and brother had carried her there, limp and wrapped in a blanket.

Mrs. Pappas pulled up a chair, took her hand, and began to speak slowly. Her voice was smooth, that of a nurse with a well-practiced bedside manner. She spoke to Penelope like an adult, in serious but comforting tones.

The fever had come fast, she explained. Penelope had complained that she was absolutely burning. Then, delirium set in briefly before she fainted with fever. Some said it was the evil eye. Mrs. Pappas thought perhaps it was Typhoid. The doctor from Tripolis had been by twice. He could do little but leave powders and instructions.

She had been lying there for two weeks. The fever had gone a day or so before, but Penelope's mind and body hadn't caught up yet.

Hearing that, she bolted upright in bed.

"No! Nurse Pappas! I have to go," she practically sobbed.

But she could only lay back down again. She was too weak to sit.

Across the world, Louis sat in silence on the train back to St. Louis, the journey itself feeling like punishment. He considered every possibility, from betrayal to tragedy, without an answer. He could not know that as the ship embarked on its journey, the person he had loved since he was a boy lay unconscious in a house so far away.

He tried to put it out of his mind by immersing himself in his work, but the silence from Koroni grew heavier each day. He wasn't sure whether he was mourning or waiting. He hated to admit it, but he was alone and scared.

It would be weeks before a letter reached him, sent air mail by a family member who could write. The letter was dated a few days before Penelope had regained consciousness.

HORIATIKI SALATA
TRADITIONAL VILLAGE SALAD

INGREDIENTS

DRESSING

- ¼ cup olive oil
- 2 tablespoons red wine vinegar
- ½ teaspoon grated onion
- Salt and black pepper, to taste

SALAD

- 1 yellow or red bell pepper, cut into strips
- 1 cucumber, sliced
- ½ red onion, sliced or cut in rounds
- 2 tomatoes, sliced and quartered
- 1 (2-inch) square of feta cheese per plate (as served in Greece), or crumbled if preferred
- 5 Kalamata olives per plate
- Mint leaves (optional)

HOW TO MAKE IT

DRESSING

1. Whisk olive oil, vinegar, grated onion, salt, and pepper in a small bowl or shake well in a corked cruet.

SALAD

1. Combine all vegetables in a large serving bowl.

2. Add dressing and toss gently.

3. Spoon onto salad plates.

4. Add olives, and mint if desired, to each plate distributing evenly.

5. Top each plate with feta.

One of the most popular dishes in all of Greece, this ubiquitous village salad gained its popularity from being lettuce-free. Diners find it to be a refreshing change from everyday salads. Top quality ingredients are a must.

Servings: 4
Prep Time: 15 minutes
Chill Time: Optional, 15 minutes
Total Time: 15–30 minutes
Adaptations/Notes: Page 167

The letter began with an apology: her father had gone through her things to find the address. They hoped it wasn't an intrusion. They wanted Louis to know that his new wife had not abandoned him. But the words carried little reassurance. He ran his finger across each line as he read. Fever, weakness. The outcome seemed so uncertain. The writer wanted him to know, to prepare himself, just in case. He felt a horrible combination of grief, relief, and worry. At least she hadn't changed her mind about joining him, but from what he read, it wasn't clear if she'd live.

Of course Penelope did survive. Otherwise, her story would be in an entirely different historical account, not here.

Recovery took time. Mrs. Pappas insisted she stay in bed, recommending six months' rest before the long journey.

Penelope didn't want to wait that long. So, with her father's help, she was re-booked a few months later, again on the S.S. Athenai, to sail from Kalamata, Greece to the United States.

A few days before the ship was to leave, she was watering the potted herbs on the rooftop.

The squeal of bicycle brakes could be heard three stories below. Watering can still in hand, she peered over the edge, The mailman stood on the gravel road below. He was reaching into the large, worn leather pouch he carried cross-body. He pulled out a letter and handed it to her grandmother.

Penelope rushed downstairs as quickly as she could, unsteady in her slippers, gripping the banister. Letters at their house were rare. Virtually all of their bills were settled in person with local merchants, who ran tabs for them. Nobody in their house could read particularly well. She hoped it wasn't bad news.

It was from Louis. He was immensely relived she had recovered, yet sorry to tell her that he didn't have enough money to make a second trip from East St. Louis to New York. He asked if she would be willing to wait a while longer. He signed it with "true hope that we are together soon."

Even though the illness couldn't be helped, Penelope felt partly responsible. Plus, she reasoned, Louis was going to need money for their new life abroad.

The humility of the words he had written had moved her. She didn't know Louis had eloquence like that because he practically never talked.

Sunday came and her family hurried off to liturgy. The priest had been by to bless Penelope's health, and had told her to rest for a while before coming back. She could recall being too weak to care during Sunday services just weeks before. Now, she longed to go somewhere, anywhere. The house felt so empty. She fidgeted in her chair, tapped her kneecap, jiggled her foot. The sunlight was casting late morning shadows on the furniture. She got up and ran her hand along the sideboard, the chair, the table, the counter. That distracted her. Soon, she would not be able to touch them anymore.

The door swung open. Her family was home. The walk from church had been chilly. She waited a while for everyone to settle.

"Baba," she called to her father. He was seated at the table, breathing in the steamy aroma from an herbal infusion in a small enamel cup he held with both hands.

She hadn't used this pet name for her father since she was little. She slid onto the stool opposite him. This was the first time she had ever discussed anything so adult-like with anyone. She explained the situation awkwardly, then fell silent and waited.

Her father answered with a tone she had only heard him use with other adults. He was business-like, and brief.

"I'll make arrangements, Peni," he told her.

She could tell he was still a little upset with her about her rejection of the Vrachonis kid.

However, he did wire what little spare cash he had so that Louis could afford to take a second trip to meet his daughter when she arrived. Whether it was to help, or to finally marry her off, she never knew.

Penelope resisted the idea of a farewell party. Not only was she still very weak, but she didn't want her father to spend any more money. But she had already talked her parents into a small, simple wedding, against their wishes. This was the last time they'd be able to celebrate their daughter. She didn't know if they'd ever see her again. So, she did it for them.

GRILLED OCTOPUS
WITH LEMON-OLIVE DRESSING (LADOLEMONO)

INGREDIENTS

- 2–2½ lb (900–1,100 g) fresh octopus, cleaned

- ½ cup (120 ml) dry red wine

- 2 bay leaves

- 10 whole black peppercorns

- ½ cup (120 ml) extra-virgin olive oil, divided

- Juice of 2 lemons

- 1 tablespoon red wine vinegar

- 1 teaspoon dried Greek oregano

- Sea salt and freshly ground pepper, to taste

HOW TO MAKE IT

1. Bring a large pot to medium heat and add octopus, wine, bay leaves, and peppercorns. Cover and cook gently in its own juices for 45–60 minutes, until tender when pierced with a fork. No water is needed; the natural juices will keep the dish succulent.

2. Remove from heat and allow to cool in the pot. Drain, reserving a few tablespoons of the cooking liquid.

3. Cut into manageable lengths (4–5 inches). Brush with olive oil and season lightly with salt and pepper.

4. Preheat an outdoor grill or cast-iron grill pan to medium-high heat. Grill octopus for 3–4 minutes per side, just until edges are crisp and lightly charred.

5. Meanwhile, whisk together the remaining olive oil, lemon juice, vinegar, and oregano to make ladolemono dressing.

6. Arrange on a serving platter, drizzle generously with ladolemono, and serve warm or at room temperature with crusty bread and a glass of white wine.

Servings: 4
Prep Time: 20 minutes
Cook Time: 55–60 minutes total
Total Time: ~1 hour 20 minutes
Adaptations/Notes: Page 167

Friends and relatives from all across town gathered at their usual spot, an abandoned lot where a house had stood long before. It had burnt to the ground in a fire nobody could recall. All that was left was the brick oven at one end, charred but intact. Everyone called it the Foúrno, which simply means "oven." Over the decades, villagers had brought benches and planted saplings they'd propagated from trees in their own yards. The place had become a neighborhood park of sorts. Now shaded and green, so many celebrations were held there that people would only need to mention if a party was not going to take place there.

Villagers came carrying plates, bottles, folding tables, bags of lemons, and plenty of coal. Penelope's father, along with a few from his game night group, started the fire. Penelope hadn't needed to ask her father to make sure nobody from the Vrachonis family would come. Everyone knew they were still offended by her refusal of that proposal.

Her brothers had brought a sturdy chair for Penelope, who still couldn't be on her feet for long. She had been bedridden for so many weeks that the smell of smouldering coals wafting across the fresh air was like life coming back into her lungs as she sat quietly and watched.

She didn't care as much for their words. There was no way to capture what lie ahead, even for her.

On board the ship the next day, Penelope had wished she could continue to wave at her smiling relatives as it left the harbor, but she was still too weak to be on her feet in the hot sun for long, so she had to leave the railing and retreat a nearby bench onboard, and watch other passengers wave as the shore gradually disappeared from view.

CHAPTER TWO

Alee

1910. NEW YORK HARBOR

Louis tried to hide his concern when he took her satchel and embraced her outside the processing building at the port. Penelope's usually healthy torso was bony and thin. Her cheeks were pale and her eyes tired and empty. On the train, he took out a tin lunch pail and unlatched it. Inside was a nickel Thermos flask, its surface dulled from handling. He twisted off the screw-top lid that doubled as a cup. Inside, a fragile glass liner was cradled in a vacuum seal, the latest invention that promised to keep broth warm for hours. A strip of worn leather was still strapped around its middle, meant to protect it on long journeys. He also produced a faded cloth handkerchief and a spoon.

"Avgolemono," he offered.

She sat silently, sipping the perfectly lemon-tinged orzo and flavorful chicken and egg broth. It was lightly frothed, just as it should be. She was too dazed to notice how much Louis' own cooking skills had improved with practice. She only knew it tasted like heaven. Or maybe like home. She didn't have the energy to think about it too deeply.

Weary tears filled her eyes as she looked through the train car's window at the lush and green, yet unfamiliar terrain moving past her, while the soup's aroma of home filled her with comfort.

1911. EAST ST. LOUIS

Years later, Penelope would tell her children that she hardly remembered her first days in the United States. She was too overwhelmed and sick to take hardly anything in. The arduous journey by boat was a setback for her, health-wise. Over time, she grew stronger, but still tired easily.

Weeks passed and she finally had the strength to go out again. A group of Greeks had been gathering at Druid's Hall just across the river to worship in their own language and faith. Their dream was that someday they could build a church of their own, but for the time being, the hall would have to do.

AVGOLEMONO SOUP
A POPULAR GREEK CLASSIC, LEMONY AND SATISFYING

INGREDIENTS

- 6 cups chicken broth (preferably homemade or low-sodium)

- 1/2 cup uncooked orzo pasta

- 3 large eggs, at room temperature

- 1/4 cup fresh lemon juice (about 2–3 lemons)

- 1/2 teaspoon kosher salt, plus more to taste

- 1/4 teaspoon freshly ground black pepper

- Fresh parsley or dill, homemade seasoned croutons, or garnish of your choice.

HOW TO MAKE IT

1. In a medium pot, bring chicken broth to a boil. Add rice (or orzo) and reduce heat to a simmer. Cook until tender, according to package instructions.

2. Prepare the egg mixture: In a medium bowl, whisk the eggs until frothy. Slowly whisk in the lemon juice until combined.

3. Temper the eggs: Ladle 1 cup of the hot broth (without rice) into a measuring cup. While whisking constantly, slowly drizzle the hot broth into the egg-lemon mixture to gently warm it without scrambling the eggs.

4. Combine: Gradually pour the tempered egg mixture back into the pot with the rice and broth, stirring constantly. Heat over low, but do not boil, until soup thickens slightly and becomes creamy, 3–5 minutes.

5. Season: Taste and adjust seasoning with additional salt and pepper.

6. Serve: Ladle into bowls and garnish if desired.

Servings: 4-6
Prep Time: 10 minutes
Cook Time: 25 minutes
Total Time: 35 minutes
Adaptations/Notes: Page 168

1911. EAST ST. LOUIS

Neither of them minded the makeshift setup. "God is everywhere," Louis used to say. The fellowship time after services provided an excellent opportunity to meet others from their homeland. Most everyone in the group was still learning English, so even the most mundane outings could be a struggle. The fellowship time after Sunday services felt so freeing. They could communicate easily. Penelope and Louis made many new friends.

There was a particularly welcoming air on those breezy afternoons in that hall. There was one group of young husbands, though, that made Penelope nervous whenever she saw them huddled together.

The men were restless. Back home, Greece was fighting the Turks again. The Peloponnese, where they had come from, had been free since the War of Independence in the 1820s, but Macedonia, Epirus, and the Aegean islands remained under Ottoman rule. In her lifetime, she had only heard distant reports of fighting hundreds of miles north of her hometown.

Every time those men got together, they'd have fiery discussions about Ottoman occupation, waving their arms and pounding the table. If one of them made a particularly powerful point, the others would cheer him on, agreeing loudly. Even though it had been seventy-five years or more since Greece had liberated themselves from that empire, there were a few cities and islands, small pockets of Greece that were still under their control.

On the streetcar ride back home that Sunday evening, she asked Louis, "Why do they feel like they need to go back and fight?"

"A new war has started," he replied. She could detect an unusual danger in the undertone of his voice. "They believe Greece should be under one rule, our own. The Ottoman empire is weak now. This is our best chance for us to take all of our country back."

Us, she thought? His explanation made Penelope even more uneasy. In the following weeks, the men spoke every Sunday of honor and duty, of family still under Ottoman rule, of the chance to reclaim what had been lost. Louis listened quietly at first, then less so. She'd watch him from across the

Louis Harrison, in his military uniform. He returned to Greece to fight against the Ottoman Empire in the Balkan war, circa 1912.

room, waving his arms animatedly as they all spoke. She could tell, the more he heard, the more his heart pulled toward the mountains and villages he had left behind.

Penelope tried to reason with him. She was only sixteen, and the idea of him leaving made her chest tighten until she could hardly breathe. They had crossed an ocean, built a fragile new beginning, and now the old world was calling him back. They had their first argument. Then, silence.

When he finally made his decision, he didn't shout it or plead his case. He simply said he had to go. The men from Druid's Hall were leaving together. They would fight for Greece, and he could not stay behind while others took up arms for their country. She wanted to be proud, but the truth was, she was terrified.

The morning he left, the mist clung to the air. She stood at the edge of the alleyway and watched her husband walk away, her face wet with something between tears and disbelief. She told herself it would only be for a short while, that he would come back, that the war would end quickly. But deep down, she knew she may never see him again.

The group of young wives were supportive to one another, but most of them lived on the St. Louis side, and Penelope didn't feel confident enough yet to take the streetcar there on her own. Without even Sunday gatherings to cheer her, she felt utterly alone.

She watched for the mail to arrive every day. Once every few weeks, there would be a letter from Koroni, and she'd write back. Yet months passed without word from Louis.

One morning, she was mopping the floors when she heard the mail fall through the slot on the front door. It landed on the damp floor. On top, she could see a handwritten letter. Leaning the mop against the fireplace, she hurried as quickly across the floor as she could without slipping.

The letter was soggy. It sort of sagged in her hand. The handwriting didn't look like Louis'. That worried her. Was he all right? She tore it open, quickly.

Koroni, May 1912

My dear Mrs. Harrison,

We have all heard that your husband has gone to fight the Turks. Such courage is admirable, although it is also dangerous work for a man so young and newly married. I would not wish harm on anyone, of course, but the truth is that few who go to war return unchanged. I myself still have nightmares of my time on the front lines.

Many do not return at all.

Please do not think me unkind for saying so. I only mean to remind you that you still have friends here who remember you fondly. Should you find yourself alone, I would consider it only right to help you secure a respectable home again.

My son, as you know, is a young man of quality, with prospects any woman would be fortunate to share. He has often said you were the finest girl in Koroni, and he would still be willing to take you as his wife, even though you are no longer untouched. There would be no need for anyone to speak of that. No one in the village would ever have to know.

I have no doubt you will see the sense in this if the time comes. In these matters, a woman must think of her future. I hope you will accept these words and my offer with the generous spirit with which I write.

With kind regards,

Anastasios Vrachonis

Penelope read the letter twice in disbelief before setting it down. The room was very quiet.

She stared at it for a long time, her hands resting flat on the table. Then she folded the pages neatly and slipped them back into the envelope, pressing the crease smooth with her thumb.

For a moment she considered throwing it into the stove, but instead she placed it in the trunk beneath her linens.

She sat for a while, listening to the clock. Then she rose, straightened the tablecloth, and went to finish the floors.

She hadn't considered being left without a husband, no longer a virgin, in a foreign country at such a young age. She felt lonelier than ever.

Several more weeks passed, then finally a letter from Louis came. The envelope was nearly destroyed, and the postmark bore a date eight weeks prior. The chalky-colored, worn stamps bore images of Hermes heads, and lettering in Greek.

Louis reported that things were going well. The journey on the SS Patri was fine. The group of men were so supportive to one another.

How wonderful, she thought sarcastically.

He said thousands of Greeks had returned from the United States to represent their home country in the Balkans.

With that, Penelope threw the letter down bitterly. She felt like he wrote it to justify abandoning her. But she didn't crumple it. Instead, she stood by the table, staring down at it. She ignored his words, but looked at the signature:

With all of my heart and soul to the one, incredible woman God gave me whom I truly adore,

Louis

Penelope thought she'd go mad. She spent her days making their house a home. She'd scour the shops for fabric and yarn on sale that she liked, then make curtains, bedspreads, blankets, table linens, anything she could to pass the time. She didn't have the heart to cook, not for herself alone.

Their small place looked cozier with her latest, homemade touches. She wondered often if Louis would ever see it.

She didn't decorate for Christmas. What was the point? One afternoon, she had idly crocheted a small, green Christmas tree with round, white ornaments and a yellow star at the top. It sat on the mantle.

She had just finished breakfast and was studying that tiny, knit tree when there was a knock at the door. Instinctively, she gathered her coin purse to pay the milkman, or whoever it was.

She wiped her hands on her apron, opened the door, and there he was, thinner, darker, the same eyes.

For a moment she couldn't speak. Louis smiled faintly and set down his small trunk. "I told you I would come back," he said.

She stepped forward and touched his sleeve. It felt coarse, unfamiliar, like another man's coat. Then she put her head on his shoulder, tucked herself against him, and for a long while neither of them spoke.

Together, they shopped and filled the home's empty pantry. That afternoon, she cooked for the first time in months. The kitchen smelled of heritage stew, and the small house seemed full again. He told her stories of ships and camps and men who never came home, but she only half-listened. Instead, she studied him to see if she could pinpoint exactly how he was different.

It wasn't long before they were expecting their first child.

Louis told his suppliers that he needed to hurry and re-open his candy shop before his wife gave birth. A few months later, he had a small grand opening. Luckily, there was little competition in the area, so the store had steady business from the start. They had a consistent income, but it required him to spend long hours there. He would arrive early and mop the floors. In the morning, the customers were mostly adults looking for gifts. He would give them a sample, and if they had time, offer them to join him at one of the three tiny tables where they would sip coffee he kept in a hidden pot in back.

The child was born, a healthy baby boy. He had Penelope's heart-shaped face. In every other way, he looked like a mini-Louis.

They named him Robert.

Louis had made many friends at the shop, but fatherhood had changed him. Those relaxed conversations, the patrons' smiles and laughter, they made him wish he was at home with Penelope instead now, watching his baby grow.

Louis and Penelope in their candy store in the East St. Louis, Illinois area circa 1915.

Later each day, he would have to repeat several times to hordes of schoolchildren filling the room that it was closing time. He'd start politely, and some of the kids would leave. Eventually, it was reduced to a "getouttahere" with a chuckle as he practically pushed the last few stragglers out the door. When he would finally lock the door, he would return to the small kitchen in the back room and make candy for the next day.

STIFADO
BRAISED BEEF HERITAGE STEW

INGREDIENTS

- 2 pounds beef stew meat, cut into 2-inch cubes

- 3 tablespoons olive oil or butter (dairy or plant-based)

- 2 medium onions, chopped (or 12–15 pearl onions, peeled)

- 3–4 cloves garlic, minced

- 2–3 tablespoons red wine vinegar

- 1 (6-ounce) can tomato paste

- 1 cup dry red wine (or substitute beef broth)

- 1 cup beef broth (in addition to the wine or 2 cups to replace it)

HOW TO MAKE IT

1. Brown the beef: In a large heavy pot or Dutch oven, heat the olive oil over medium-high. Add the beef in batches and brown well on all sides, 6–8 minutes. Adjust cooking time when subsituting other proteins. Remove to a plate.

2. Sauté the onions: In the same pot, add onions and cook until softened and lightly golden, 5–7 minutes.

Add garlic and cook 1 minute more.

3. Deglaze: Stir in the wine vinegar, scraping up any browned bits.

4. Add remaining liquids and seasoning: Return beef to the pot. Add tomato paste, red wine, beef broth, cloves, bay leaves, cinnamon stick (if using), oregano, salt, and pepper. Stir well to combine.

5. Simmer: Bring to a boil, then reduce heat to low. Cover and simmer gently until the beef is very tender, about 2 hours. Check occasionally and add a splash more broth if needed.

6. Finish: Remove bay leaves, cloves, and cinnamon stick. Adjust seasoning to taste.

7. Serve: Garnish with fresh parsley. Serve hot over hilopites (tagliatelle if hilopites isn't available, gluten-free pasta or rice)

Servings: 6
Prep Time: 20 minutes
Cook Time: 2 hours 30 minutes
Total Time: 2 hours 50 minutes
Adaptations/Notes: Page 168

At home, Penelope would wake alone to frost on the windows. Robert was growing quickly. Penelope was strong, but soon he'd be too big for her to lift.

Tiptoeing, she'd try to dress before she heard the baby stirring in his bassinet. She would bundle him in blankets and carry him through the drafty hallway into the tiny kitchen to feed him. She hardly ate herself. She didn't have the energy to cook or even to shop.

Louis would bring home a loaf of bread, some cheese and olives. The two of them would sip wine and eat. Still in love, but exhausted.

It wasn't until Robert was around six months old that Penelope felt some of her energy returning. He was sleeping the night, and napping well during the day. Finally, she was strong enough to shop for groceries and cook real meals.

It was then, with her husband's help, Mrs. Penelope Stamatelos-Harrison developed skills that would eventually make her the best cook anyone in her social circle had ever encountered. During those long afternoons alone at home, while Robert napped and Louis was working, she chopped parsley, crumbled feta and drizzled complex sauces over perfectly cooked meat and vegetables. With each preparation, her craft began to improve.

The deliciousness of their evening meals cast a welcome, warm light over the bleak St. Louis winter. Things seemed to be getting better.

Behind Louis' quiet nature, Penelope discovered a rich and complicated mind, quick to notice what others overlooked. What had once seemed like shyness began to look more like patience. With immigration, combat, the building of a business, and the starting of a family all behind him, he seemed to look at life differently now. His withdrawn nature was undetectable. His boyishness would surface now and then, but always in the right context, like when he was speaking to the older children who liked to hang around in his shop.

Louis was resourceful, and, as he grew comfortable, unexpectedly jovial. People respected him.

Things felt more stable, but still far from easy. Neither of them was accustomed to the chilly Midwestern winters. Life in Greece had been sunny and warm. Also tranquil. The city in the wintertime seemed enormous, frigid, and noisy around them.

Life in those first few decades of the century was unpredictable. When Penelope learned she was expecting their second child in 1916, she and Louis felt the house fill with a kind of joy that felt new; unfamiliar to either of them. They wondered if they would have a girl this time. They watched baby Robert play, and imagined two instead of one.

But joy can turn quickly. Robert's illness came suddenly, first a fever, then he could hardly stand. His tiny body fought, yet he grew weaker. Penelope sat by his crib through long nights, listening for each shallow breath. She held her rosary in one hand and let his tiny hand rest curled around one of her fingers with the other. She whispered prayers that grew more desperate as the days passed. Louis paced the floors, fetching water, calling for the doctor, trying to hide the fear in his eyes.

They watched helplessly as their baby slipped further away, until the house that had once been filled with tiny cries and baby laughter fell into silence.

Robert was gone.

The rooms felt unbearably large. The time passed unbearably slowly. The tiny linens folded with such care days before were left untouched. The floorboards were freezing. Every step stung Penelope's feet, as sharply as every tear burned her face. She would allow them to flow while Louis was at work, while Louis' own tears fell after he closed himself into the back room of the candy store in the early evenings and late nights.

Neighbors offered condolences, food, prayers, but nothing could lift the weight of the emptiness.

1917. GREEK INDEPENDENCE DAY

It was Penelope's first outing since the birth of her second child, a girl they named Agalaia. She sat next to Louis on the streetcar with the baby in her arms, wrapped in blankets. He tucked at her coat and the baby's blanket occasionally to make sure they were both covered and warm. The baby was exactly one month old that day.

They were on their way to Druid's Hall. They hadn't been there in months. Penelope had been pregnant, then had the child. It was her first time since Louis had returned.

She looked down at her daughter. The baby looked back up at her mother with bright, curious eyes. Penelope wanted to bask in the glow of her beauty, like she had with Robert. But the gray day made her feel so tired. She had two, but held just one.

Her mood made her realize how deeply she needed time for meditation and prayer. The day ahead was an exciting one for the area's growing, Greek community. After the service, the women would prepare a meal in the hall while the men held a meeting. The topic was the planning of the first Greek Orthodox church in the region. A place to worship of their own.

9th & Market. He held the baby as he helped her step down. They walked to the hall. Inside, she took Aglaia back from him and looked around. She was relived to find that the atmosphere was completely different than the last time she had been there. There was no talk of war. No tension in the air.

After the service, Louis took a seat in one of the last rows. He held Aglaia in his arms, who was sleeping peacefully now. The planning meeting began.

BAKALIAROS SKORDALIÁ
FRIED COD WITH GARLIC PURÉE

INGREDIENTS

MAIN DISH

*   2 pounds salted cod fillets (or fresh cod, lightly salted)

    1 ½ cups all-purpose flour (or gluten-free flour blend for adaptation)

    1 teaspoon baking powder

    1 cup cold sparkling water (or beer, for a regional variation)

    Olive oil, for frying

FOR THE SKORDALIÁ

See page 73 for Nickolas' recipe. This can be prepared in advance.

HOW TO MAKE IT

1. Prepare the Skordaliá according to the directions on page 73.

2. Prepare the main dish:
    Rinse the salted cod thoroughly, then soak in cold water for 24 hours, changing the water 2–3 times. Drain, pat dry, and cut into serving-size pieces.

3. Make the batter:
    In a mixing bowl, whisk flour, baking powder, and sparkling water until smooth. The batter should lightly coat the back of a spoon. Chill 10–15 minutes.

4. Fry the cod:
    Heat olive oil in a deep skillet over medium-high heat. Dip cod pieces in batter and fry until golden and crisp on all sides, about 4–5 minutes per side. Drain on paper towels.

    Serve:
    Serve hot with Skordaliá on the side, lemon wedges, and a drizzle of olive oil.

An exotic twist on classic fish and chips. If using salted cod (bakaliaros), soak it for 48 to 72 hours, changing the water several times per day. That step is unnecessary if using fresh cod.

Servings: 6
Prep Time: 25 minutes
Cook Time: 25 minutes
Total Time: 50 minutes
Adaptations/Notes: Page 169

Penelope went into the commercial kitchen, where rows of Greek grandmothers were expertly prepping at the long, stainless-steel countertop. What she saw gave her a sudden, vivid flashback to life in Koroni, a déjà vu. She watched their capable hands in wonder as they pressed garlic with mortars and pestles, efficiently whisked flour, baking powder, and beer in tin bowls, rinsed piece after piece of cod and dredged them in the batter.

She blinked and came back to herself. A few of the younger women she knew were gathered over a large metal tin, peeling potatoes, so she joined them. That day, the others probably peeled triple the potatoes Penelope did. She worked at a glacier's pace, more intent on watching the entire process than keeping pace. The repetition of movement, the smell of frying fish, the laughter. It filled her with a sense of belonging she hadn't felt in years.

When they finally sat down to eat, the fried cod and garlic purée (Bakaliaros Skordaliá) tasted like memory itself. Crisp, tangy, simple, perfect. For Penelope, it was more than a meal. It was the moment she understood that cooking wasn't just about feeding others. It was a way back.

They lingered long after the meal, but in time Aglaia was quietly fussing, so she motioned to Louis that she was going to duck into a side room for a while. He nodded, and she found a quiet place to feed her. When the baby finally fell asleep, she rose slowly, careful not to disturb her.

The air in the main hall felt unexpectedly uncomfortable when she stepped through the wide doorway. The easy warmth from before was gone. Just as before Louis had left for war, the young men were deep in discussion. It looked serious. She wondered what they could possibly be discussing now. A faint, familiar pulse of anxiety moved through her body.

On the ride home, Louis was excited about the plans for a new church. Instead of mentioning anything about war, he recounted every detail that had been discussed in the planning meeting. Penelope tried her best to listen, but she was so tired from being on her feet all day. She didn't have the energy to ask him about the conversation they had afterward.

The two of them had eaten such a large lunch that they were not hungry for dinner. Penelope poured olive oil into a small pan and heated some finely chopped garlic. Taking it off the heat, she spooned in a small amount of tomato paste and added salt, ground pepper and oregano. She stirred it well, then poured it onto a saucer. The two of them dipped bread in it and picked at a small bowl of Kalamata olives. She poured a small glass of wine for Louis, but she didn't want any.

After they had finished, she rose from the table to clear the dishes.

Suddenly, she dropped a plate, the loud shatter startling her so much she froze. She squeezed her eyes shut, bracing for anger, sharp words about carelessness.

Instead, Louis only laughed softly, bent down, and began gathering the pieces with her, his large hands steadying hers. "It's only a plate," he said, as if plates could be replaced and she could not. "You didn't cut yourself, did you?"

He was kneeling. His hand still held jagged shards of plate.

LADI KAI TOMATA
FIVE-MINUTE TOMATO DIPPING OIL

INGREDIENTS

- ¼ cup extra-virgin olive oil
- 1 garlic clove, finely chopped
- 1 tablespoon tomato paste
- ½ teaspoon dried oregano
- Pinch of sea salt
- Freshly ground black pepper, to taste
- Crusty bread or Kalamata olives, for serving

HOW TO MAKE IT

1. In a small pan, gently heat the olive oil over low flame. Add chopped garlic and cook until fragrant, about 30 seconds. Do not let it brown.

2. Remove from heat. Stir in tomato paste, oregano, salt, and pepper until smooth and slightly thickened.

3. Spoon onto a shallow saucer and let cool slightly before serving.

4. Serve warm or at room temperature, with fresh bread for dipping and olives alongside.

Servings: 2
Prep Time: 3 minutes
Cook Time: 2 minutes
Total Time: 5 minutes
Adaptations/Notes: Page 169

She looked at her husband. His face was kind but he was furrowing his young brow. He wasn't trying to stifle frustration and act patient. No, she felt it. He was genuinely concerned. Not for the plate, for her.

In that very moment, their bond, which had wobbled back and forth like a pinball, finally evolved into something far deeper. This was the man who would protect her, who would never shame her. The one who would build a life with her in all the small moments, and all the big ones too.

Penelope turned her head. She didn't want Louis to see her crying, but he knew.

"What is it, my dear?" He asked her.

They stood up and threw the rest of the broken plate pieces away. Then, he leaned against the counter and looked at her.

"Is something wrong?"

She didn't want to upset him, but fear got the best of her. She asked what the men had been discussing so intently at the end of the evening. She was nervous, so she overexplained, mentioning how she had noticed their faces, how she just knew it was something, and how he should just tell her.

"Are you planning on leaving again, Louie?"

It took him a moment to grasp her meaning. His expression softened slowly, as if he were trying to decide whether to laugh. When he finally did, it started quiet, then turned into full, helpless laughter.

She stared, caught between offense and confusion.

"What's so funny?" she asked.

He reached out and rested his hand lightly on her upper arm. "Sit for a minute."

She did, not entirely sure if she should be more worried now than before.

"Some of the men," he began, "their fathers knew the elder Vrachonis brothers from the war."

She stiffened, unsure where this was going. "The war?"

He nodded, the faintest smile still tugging at his mouth. "Everyone knew they never saw a day of combat. Guard duty, supply routes. They came home talking like generals."

She blinked, realizing he was serious.

He went on. "And before you start thinking they were the heroes they claimed to be, I should tell you something."

Her stomach tightened. "What?"

He looked straight at her. "I knew about it. The boy. The one you refused to marry."

Her breath caught. For a moment, she forgot to look away.

"I grew up quiet," he said. "That doesn't mean I didn't have ears."

She tried to speak but couldn't.

He leaned forward slightly, his tone turning warm. "When I heard you said no, I said a little prayer in my room that night. I already liked you, but that sealed it. Anyone who could turn down a Vrachonis with that much confidence deserved better company."

There was a silence. The type that fills a room when truth settles in.

Then she smiled, slow and disbelieving. "You prayed?"

He shrugged, pretending not to notice her grin. "I didn't trust the kid either."

She laughed then, softly at first, then enough that it made him join in. It was the kind of laughter that came from years of misunderstanding and relief all at once.

She walked over to the shelf and pulled the letter she had received from underneath the linens and showed it to him. The disbelief on Louis' face that evening was something the two laughed about for years after.

CHAPTER THREE

Oceans are Consciousness in Dreams

EARLY 1917. PIRAEUS HARBOR, GREECE

Halfway across the globe, the S.S. Vasilefs Constantinos let out a prolonged blast of its whistle to indicate it was leaving port. On board was a couple, Kyrios Thomas and Kyria Maria Tsetsos, with their four-year-old child Nickolas. Both the child's name, and its traditional Greek spelling, originated from their hometown of St. Nickolas, Greece.

For their trip, they had booked meager accommodations; Third Class (Steerage) with dormitory-style rooms, the most basic of meals, and little privacy. It was the best they could do. Although the child was almost of school age, he was still breast-feeding because they couldn't afford milk.

Passengers board the SS Vasilefs Constantinos in Piraeus, Greece, 1917, as a crewmember looks on.

The journey was long, and the seas rough due to unexpected spells of rain and wind along the way. Since it was a shared cabin, the door was opened and closed constantly. The room was always damp. When the sun went down, it was very cold. The three of them lacked clothing warm enough to be comfortable, so they huddled together with the child between them night after night.

There were countless immigrants on that voyage. To the shipping company and United States Immigration officials, they were names on a manifest. But each hand that held a pen to sign a document belonged to someone who had just been on the longest journey of their life, with an even longer one ahead.

The hope they had felt upon departure, the dreams of a new homeland, were put on hold. The ship made stop after stop. Kalamata and Patras in Greece, Palermo in Sicily, then onto coaling and provisioning in the Portuguese Azores. With each docking, the delays began to stack up. The Azores stop was the last glimpse of land the passengers saw before the long push to America. Then, all that lie ahead was a seemingly endless horizon. Nothing but sea and gray skies.

A souvenir postcard depicting the SS Vasilefs Constantinos in rough seas.

Three weeks later, the ship reached New York. All went their separate ways, traveling far and wide, probably to all forty-eight states. However, this young family's journey was far from over. The train ride across country was arduous. They had only seats, not a place to sleep, and they were given just one meal a day. Finally, they arrived at their final destination; Los Angeles.

The S.S. Vasilefs Constantinos left port and returned to Greece. World War I was in full swing. By that time, the Allies had occupied parts of Greece and were using their ports for their war efforts. The very ship that brought them across the Atlantic was torpedoed by a German Navy submarine and sunk into the Mediterranean Sea just weeks after they had been aboard. The news reached Kyrios Thomas through acquaintances. He viewed it as a sign from God that they would have metaphorically "sunk to the bottom of the ocean" if they had stayed in the old country. During Sunday church services, he silently said prayers of thanks for his family's survival, and for their new life in America. Yet, he never told his wife and son about the ship's tragic end. He didn't want to upset them.

1917. CITY OF ANGELS

Los Angeles was a bustling, rapidly-growing city. As the Tsetsos family stepped off the train and flagged a cab down to take them on the short ride to the home of a distant relative, they watched in wonder. The city stretched wide, low, and busy, with broad streets full of electric streetcars and a surprising number of automobiles. There were rows of brick and stone buildings downtown, new hotels and banks opening, and neon signs just beginning to appear. The air carried the smell of orange blossoms from the nearby groves, mixed with sawdust from construction, which seemed to be going on everywhere. It was nothing like Greece, and not like anything they had seen on their ride across the country.

FASOLADA SOUP
CONSIDERED BY MANY TO BE THE NATIONAL DISH OF GREECE

INGREDIENTS

- 1 pound dried white beans (navy beans or cannellini), soaked overnight and drained

- 1/4 cup olive oil

- 1 large onion, chopped

- 2 carrots, diced

- 2 celery stalks, diced

- 3–4 garlic cloves, minced

- 1 (15-ounce) can crushed tomatoes, or 2 tablespoons tomato paste diluted in 1 cup water

- 2 bay leaves

- 1 teaspoon dried oregano

- 1 1/2 teaspoons salt, plus more to taste

- 5–6 whole cloves

HOW TO MAKE IT

1. Prepare beans: If you haven't soaked the beans overnight, use the quick-soak method: cover beans with water in a large pot, bring to a boil, then turn off heat and let sit 1 hour. Drain before cooking.

2. Sauté aromatics: In a large soup pot, heat the olive oil over medium heat. Add onion, carrots, and celery. Cook until softened, 6–8 minutes. Stir in

garlic and cook 1 minute more.

3. Add beans and liquid: Stir in beans, crushed tomatoes (or tomato paste mixture), bay leaves, oregano, salt, and pepper. Add water or broth.

4. Simmer: Bring to a boil, then reduce heat to low. Simmer gently, partially covered, until beans are tender and soup has thickened, 60–75 minutes. Stir occasionally and add more liquid if needed.

5. Finish: Remove bay leaves. Taste and adjust seasoning.

6. Serve: Ladle into bowls, drizzle with additional olive oil, and serve with crusty bread.

Kyria Maria made large quantities to serve her patrons. This soup was immensely popular as a lunch item. It was reasonable in cost, healthy, delicious and very satisfying.

Servings: 6-8
Prep Time: 15 minutes (plus overnight soaking)
Cook Time: 1 hour 30 minutes
Total Time: About 1 hour 45 minutes (plus soaking time)
Adaptations/Notes: Page 170

Even five-year-old Nickolas would never forget that day. He watched in awe, as the builders bellowed at one another standing high up on beams as they worked.

Kyrios Thomas and Kyria Maria Tsetsos opened their own general store in Los Angeles. It stocked provisions, some groceries and feed for livestock and other animals. It also had a lunch counter. On all but Sundays, Kyria Maria would make extra amounts of the daily special so that there would be enough to take home to the family for dinner.

They lived simply, scraping by.

1928. TSETSOS GENERAL STORE

Their dream was that their son Nickolas would get an education. The day after his acceptance letter to USC's School of Dentistry arrived, Kyria Maria closed the blinds in the front windows of the store from noon to one. Discreetly, they waved their regular customers right past the "closed" sign and welcomed them inside.

The place filled with laughter. Trays of food lined the lunch counter. Prohibition was in full swing, but the general store became a speakeasy for 60 minutes that day. The room filled with the clink of coffee mugs brimming with Ouzo, and shouts of "Yasou!" Some knew what they were drinking and what the word meant. Others hadn't a clue.

Everyone's joyful shouts lingered in the rafters long after the mugs were emptied. Outside, the sign still said closed, but from within came the sound of Greece and America celebrating the same dream.

Kyrios Thomas raised his glass and thanked their customers,

Kyria Maria Tsetsos behind the lunch counter of the shop she owned with her husband, Kyrios Thomas in Los Angeles. The photo is undated, circa 1920.

recognizing that their loyalty had made this day possible. Nickolas stood next and echoed his father's gratitude. One toast followed another, each wishing the future dentist luck and reminding him, amid the laughter, to always remember to brush his teeth.

CHICKEN KAPAMA
BRAISED AND SERVED IN A RICH TOMATO SAUCE

INGREDIENTS

- 1 whole chicken (about 4 pounds), cut into serving pieces

- 3 tablespoons olive oil

- 1 large onion, finely chopped

- 2 cloves garlic, minced

- 1 (15-ounce) can crushed tomatoes

- 2 tablespoons tomato paste

- 1 cup chicken stock or water

- ~1 cinnamon stick

- 2 whole cloves

- ½ teaspoon ground allspice

- 1 bay leaf

- 2 teaspoons salt

- ½ teaspoon freshly ground black pepper

- ½ cup dry red wine

HOW TO MAKE IT

1. Brown the chicken: In a wide, heavy pot, heat olive oil over medium-high heat. Add chicken pieces and brown well on all sides. Remove and set aside.

2. Sauté aromatics: In the same pot, add onion and garlic. Sauté until golden, about 4–5 minutes.

3. Build the sauce: Stir in crushed tomatoes, tomato paste, chicken stock, wine, cinnamon stick, cloves, allspice, bay leaf, salt, and pepper. Mix well.

4. Simmer: Return the chicken to the pot, turning pieces to coat in the sauce. Bring to a gentle boil, then reduce heat to low. Cover and simmer for 1 hour, stirring occasionally, until the chicken is tender and the sauce is thickened.

5. Serve: Discard the bay leaf and cinnamon stick. Serve warm over orzo, rice, or mashed potatoes, spooning the rich cinnamon-tomato sauce over each serving.

Your secret ingredient here is cinnamon. Be sure to be very subtle with it, and your guests will wonder why this dish has a delicious signature taste. But only the most experienced pallets will be able to tell exactly what it is. Some serve it with feta or even parmesan over the top. Penelope didn't think it needed any topping, and I agree.

Servings: 6
Prep Time: 20 minutes
Cook Time: 1 hour 20 minutes
Total Time: 1 hour 40 minutes
Adaptations/Notes: Page 170

CHAPTER FOUR

O Amerikános

1935. JUST SOUTH OF DOWNTOWN LOS ANGELES

Nickolas was hard-working like his parents, but the apparent similarities ended there. They were solemn, reserved. He, gregarious. He would pat the backs of friends vigorously while shaking their hands whenever he gathered with them. Which was often.

He was twenty-two when prohibition finally ended. There was a brand-new drink making the rounds in the Los Angeles social circles. They were mixing Seagram's 7 Crown whiskey with 7-Up.

Prohibition repeal had come like a valve hissing open. Standing on the sidewalk on Spring Street, Nickolas pulled a small scrap of paper out of his pocket and double-checked the address. 326½ S. Spring St.

This is it, he thought to himself. He opened the heavy door wnd stepped from the blindingly bright outdoors into near-pitch-blackness. As his eyes adjusted and he scanned the room for his friends, a clarinet squeaked, and bottles thudded onto the bartop. He straightened his tie and took a seat with his friends at the bar. It still felt like they shouldn't be there.

He knew what he was going to drink before he sat down. He wanted to try that new mix everyone was talking about. As he ordered, the bartender looked at him knowingly, as if he spoke a secret,code. He placed the small, square napkin in front of Nickolas as he said cooly, "Here you are, hep cat."

"Jeffries & Kipper," was printed on it in deco letters, modern for the time. Underneath, in block print, it said, "the swellest in the USA."

The bartender set the glass down. Ice clinked against the highball. He took a sip. Sweet, bright, easy. It tasted like prohibition hadn't been the "sin" the propaganda had made it out to be. It became his favorite.

The drink that was later nicknamed the Seven and Seven became his go-to for life.

SPEAKEASY STYLE SEVEN AND SEVEN

SERVED IN A HIGHBALL GLASS WITH PLENTY OF ICE

INGREDIENTS

- 2 oz modern Seagram's 7 Crown

- ¼ oz rye whiskey [1]

- ½ tsp rich cane sugar syrup (to mimic the natural depth of old bottling)

- 1–2 drops citric acid solution (for the sharper tang of pre-1950 7-Up)

- 4–6 oz cane sug r–sweetened 7-Up ("Mexican 7-Up" or Throwback)[2]

- Cracked ice

HOW TO MAKE IT

1. Fill a highball glass with cracked ice.

2. Combine Seagram's 7 and rye whiskey.

3. Stir in cane syrup and citric acid solution.

4. Top with cane sugar–sweetened 7-Up. Stir gently.

5. Serve plain, no garnish.

[1] In the 1940s, Seagram's 7 Crown was heavier on the whiskey notes. It was still smooth and light compared to bourbon, which is why it mixed well. Today, Seagram's 7 is still a blended whiskey, but the recipe has been adjusted over the years. It's somewhat lighter, more neutral, less grain-forward than the 1940s bottlings. This is why rye whiskey is added, to boost the grainy backbone.

[2] Back then, 7-Up was made with real sugar (cane sugar or beet sugar, depending on the bottler). It had more tang from the original lemon-lime oil mix, and it contained lithium citrate until 1950, which gave it a slight medicinal edge. Nowadays, the 7-Up sold in the United States is sweetened with high-fructose corn syrup. The flavor is distinctly different than the original. For authenticity, use Mexican or Throwback 7-up. Both are available online.

Servings: 1
Prep Time: 5 minutes
Cook Time: 0 minutes
Total Time: 5 minutes
Adaptations/Notes: Page 171

He had lived in California since he was five years old. His English carried no trace of an accent. His parents both recognized and didn't, this living form of their dream of a better life. One they had held since the day they decided to leave their home country. They still knew him, still recognized Nickolas. He was fully Greek to them. Still, it was surreal to them at times, this easy American confidence. Their only son had become everything they had hoped for, in ways they couldn't have ever imagined.

Kyrios Thomas, for his part, had come to love cheeseburgers and big-band music.

While he was in dental school, Nickolas sold insurance for extra cash. It was commission-based. If he didn't sell policies, he earned nothing.

It didn't take long for him to figure out that knocking on doors didn't work well. A housewife in the middle of vacuuming the living room while her husband was at the office and the kids were in school was not about to drop an entire month's wages on homeowner's coverage. He felt like the polite rejections were sometimes more humiliating than a slammed door in the face.

Unable to find any other work that aligned with his busy school schedule, Nickolas began visiting any connections he or his family had in the small Greek community that had settled in the Los Angeles area. Friends of friends, anybody who would talk to him, he would visit.

Even though many of them didn't read English, he was able to communicate the importance of insuring important items to a group of people who couldn't afford to replace them on their own if they were damaged or lost.

Even those who weren't interested were kind. Any visitor born in their home country was a houseguest, whether they knew Nickolas personally or not. He'd be given a cup of strong Greek coffee, and maybe a small pastry,. Koulourakia were his favorite.

KOULOURAKIA

BELLE'S RECIPE

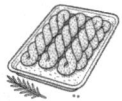

INGREDIENTS

- ½ lb. unsalted, plant-based butter, softened
- 1 cup vegetable, or other neutral oil)
- 3 cups powdered sugar
- 4 eggs
- 3 tsp vanilla extract
- 1 box + 2 cups Swan's Down cake flour
- 3 tsp baking powder

HOW TO MAKE IT

1. Preheat oven to 350°F.

2. Sift cake flour and baking powder together in a medium bowl.

3. In a separate large bowl, beat butter, oil, powdered sugar, eggs, and vanilla until smooth and creamy.

4. Gradually add sifted flour mixture to wet ingredients, mixing until dough is soft but holds its shape.

5. Shape dough into small circles or braided twists. Place on a nonstick baking sheet, or one lightly brushed with olive oil

6. Brush on melted plant-based butter and lightly sprinkle with toasted sesame seeds.

7. Bake until bottoms are lightly browned, about 15–20 minutes.

8. Cool on wire racks.

Servings: About 36 cookies (depending on size and shape)
Prep Time: 25 minutes
Cook Time: 15-20 minutes
Total Time: 40-45 minutes
Adaptations/Notes: Page 171

Nickolas got to know many Greek-American immigrants that way. Later, when he finished dental school, many of them would become his clients.

He had just started his sophomore year. That semester, he didn't have classes on Fridays. Usually, he'd be knocking on doors, but this Friday his parents needed him to work in the store for a couple of hours.

The lunch rush was just about over, when a tanned, wrinkled old man walked in and sat at the counter.

"Where is Maria?" The man asked, his accent heavy, his voice rasped by years of smoke and storytelling.

"My mother had an appointment, sir. What can I get you?"

"And Thomas?"

"My father drove her."

"You speak Greek?"

Nickolas answered that he did. The man's shoulders eased. He introduced himself as Giorgios and ordered his lunch.

FAKÈS SOUPA
HEARTY, NUTRITIOUS STAPLE OF MEDITERRANEAN CUISINE

INGREDIENTS

- 1 pound dried brown or green lentils, rinsed
- 1/4 cup olive oil
- 1 medium onion, chopped
- 2 carrots, diced
- 2–3 garlic cloves, minced
- 2 medium tomatoes, chopped (or 1 cup canned tomatoes)
- 2 bay leaves
- 1 teaspoon dried oregano
- 1 1/2 teaspoons salt, plus more to taste
- 1/2 teaspoon freshly ground black pepper
- 8 cups water or vegetable broth
- 2–3 tablespoons red wine vinegar (to finish)

HOW TO MAKE IT

1. Sauté vegetables: In a large soup pot, heat olive oil over medium heat. Add onion and carrots. Cook until softened, 5–7 minutes. Stir in garlic and cook 1 minute more.

2. Add lentils and liquid: Stir in lentils, tomatoes, bay leaves, oregano, salt, pepper, and water or broth. Bring to a boil.

3. Simmer: Reduce heat to low, cover, and simmer gently until lentils are tender and soup has thickened, about 45–60 minutes. Stir occasionally.

4. Finish: Remove bay leaves. Stir in red wine vinegar to brighten the flavor. Adjust seasoning to taste.

5. Serve: Ladle hot into bowls, with rustic sesame bread and olives on the side. Garnish with mascarpone cheese, sour cream or plant-based mozzarella.

Servings: 6-8
Prep Time: 15 minutes
Cook Time: 1 hour
Total Time: 1 hour 15 minutes
Adaptations/Notes: Page 172

Nickolas set the plate down in front of him. As the last customers left, the two of them were alone. Giorgios' eyes were bright and his voice grew livelier with each bite, his hands moving as he spoke.

"There were no Greeks in Los Angeles when my brother and I came with our father from Cephalonia forty years ago," he said in working-class Greek. "My brother was nine. I was five."

"Only five," Nickolas said thoughtfully, "that's the same age I was when I came over."

Giorgios' eyes softened.

They had lost their father to a work accident, then it was just he and his brother. Although he was only ten then, both worked as laborers and had somehow managed to survive on the streets of Los Angeles. His brother had just passed away last year.

"Your parents remember my brother," he said distantly. "The two of us used to eat lunch here."

Now, it was just him. But Georgios blew a kiss to the heavens.

"Thank goodness all of our countrymen started coming over. I wish my dear father could see what a community we have. So many Greeks now! Even though I don't have any family left here, I feel like I have family everywhere. You see, I already knew the ropes when all the other Greeks came. "When someone needed work, they said, 'talk to Giorgios.' When they needed to learn to drive, same thing. I met everybody that way. I don't think there's a Greek in town I haven't met."

He pushed aside his plate. "What do you do, son? I never saw you in here."

Nickolas told him about dental school.

"Niiiice. I'll tell everybody there's gonna be a Greek dentist," he said, "they'll all go to you." He smiled.

Then Nickolas mentioned selling insurance. "It's tough," he said, "but I can't find anything else I can do while I'm in school."

Giorgios studied him for a long time, apparently thinking. Then he said, "Lake Elsinore."

He paused, then nodded, and said it again, "Yeah, Lake Elsinore."

"Your father got a car. Borrow daddy's car, son. Drive out there. That's the spot for you. There's a widow, Mrs. Kanakis. You can stay with her. Tell her Theo Giorgios sent you. There are lotta Greeks out there, plenty of 'em. You'll sell a half-dozen of your policies, maybe more."

Considering the highway system around 1936, it would be a five to six-hour trip. Today, with modern interstates, it would be half that.

Mrs. Kanakis lived alone on a large ranch. Taking somewhat of a chance, Nickolas allowed Giorgios to use the store's telephone to talk to her. He hoped his parents wouldn't mind the long-distance call.

She answered and, after a short catch-up chat, told Giorgios she would happily let Nickolas stay the night.

If he could sell some insurance there, it would be well worth it. He decided to go.

CHAPTER FIVE

Where Ye Have Not Labored

1936. LAKE ELSINORE, CALIFORNIA

Mrs. Kanakis was lovely. She was elderly, but had a certain elegance. He pulled up to the farmhouse. It was two stories high with wide porches shaded by vines. A long driveway lined with walnut and almond trees led to its broad front steps.

She answered the door wearing wire-rimmed glasses. Her silvery hair was brushed back, away from her face, held with small combs made of seashell. Her face did show its age, but still had a fine, delicate bone structure. Her dress was black. Widows back then never publicly wore anything but black after the loss of their husband. A gesture of permanent respect and mourning. But she was not dour, and greeted him with a small, welcoming smile.

She invited Nickolas into the parlor. It had thick area rugs, oak furniture, and a gilt-framed icon of the Virgin and Child above the mantel. Lace runners embroidered by hand rested under vases of fresh flowers. On the walls, family portraits from Athens hung alongside sepia-toned photographs of her late husband in America. Nickolas wished he had brought his parents along so that they could see it too. He knew he'd never be able to do it justice with a verbal description.

Her kitchen was modern for the time, with a gas range and an icebox, yet the air was thick with the aroma of cinnamon, clove, and simmered tomato, the scents of old-world Greece.

Copper pots hung from hooks, and a well-worn bríki sat on the stove, ready for strong coffee. On the counter, beside a bowl of oranges from her orchard, sat a polished brass bowl filled with olives.

Mrs. Kanakis interrupted Nickolas' thoughts gently with a request:

«Νικόλα, παιδί μου, αν δεν σου κάνει κόπο, φέρε μου από τη πίσω βεράντα το τελάρο με τις μελιτζάνες που άφησε το πρωί ο μπακάλης. Είναι βαρύ για μένα.»

OVEN ROASTED CHICKEN LEMONÁTO
WITH GREEK POTATOES

INGREDIENTS

- 1 whole chicken (about 4–5 pounds)
- 3–4 potatoes, peeled and cut into wedges
- 1/4 cup olive oil
- Juice of 2 lemons
- 4–5 garlic cloves, chopped
- 1 tablespoon dried oregano
- 1 teaspoon salt
- 1/2 teaspoon black pepper
- 1/2 cup water

HOW TO MAKE IT

1. Heat oven to 350°F.

2. Place chicken in a large roasting pan. Scatter potato wedges around it and drizzle the olive oil over the top.

3. In a small bowl, mix, garlic, oregano, salt, and pepper. Rub this over the chicken and potatoes, making sure everything is coated well so that it crisps the chicken skin.

4. Add 1/2 cup water to the bottom of the pan.

5. Roast uncovered about 1 1/2 hours, or until chicken is golden brown and juices run clear. Apply the lemon juice after an hour or so. Baste once or twice with the pan juices.

6. Let rest 10 minutes before carving. Serve with the potatoes and the lemony pan sauce spooned over the top.

Servings: 4
Prep Time: 15 minutes
Cook Time: ~1 hour 30 minutes
Total Time: ~1 hour 45 minutes
Adaptations/Notes: Page 172

"Nickolas, my dear child, if it's not a bother to you, please bring me the basket of eggplants that the grocer left this morning from the back porch. It's heavy for me."

Nickolas opened the back door and looked out. There was an orchard, a white, embellished iron bench, and beautiful, well-kept flowerbeds. He later learned that although Mrs. Kanakis employed several farm helpers, she still preferred to do most things herself indoors. Aside from a cleaning lady who tended to the house and the laundry, she had no maids or butlers.

From the back porch, several other ranches were within view. None were as impressive as the Kanakis property, but they were all tidy, and all within walking distance. He would set out in the morning.

He picked up the basket and gently placed it where Mrs. Kanakis was gratefully pointing, in an empty spot on the floor in the back pantry. She turned and smiled, and told him that dinner was ready.

Dinner was fakés soup, followed by Greek roasted chicken and fresh vegetables. There was fresh sesame bread on the side, still hot from the oven.

During the meal, Mrs. Kanakis politely asked Nickolas questions about school and his other activities. He asked her about her own history and life on the ranch. They spoke in Greek, which impressed her. She marveled at how completely bilingual he was. His English must be close to perfect, if he was able to pass his courses, yet his Greek was excellent too. She knew the struggles other parents had when they immigrated. Some children just didn't manage to hold on to the language. Nickolas' parents had done well, she thought to herself.

As they were finishing their last few bites, Mrs. Kanakis gave him the names and locations of several Greek families nearby. She mentioned that they would be busy tending to their farms in the morning, and suggested he visit after noon. She winked, and said to tell them, "Mrs. Kanakis sent you."

PSOMI ME SOUSAMI
GREEK VILLAGE BREAD WITH SESAME SEEDS

INGREDIENTS

- 4 cups bread flour (plus more for kneading)

- 2 teaspoons salt

- 1 tablespoon sugar or honey

- 1 packet (2 ¼ teaspoons) active dry yeast

- 1 ½ cups warm water (110°F / 43°C)

- 2 tablespoons olive oil

- 1 egg white, lightly beaten (for glaze)

- 1/3 cup sesame seeds

HOW TO MAKE IT

1. Activate yeast: In a large bowl, dissolve sugar (or honey) in warm water. Sprinkle in yeast and let sit until foamy, about 5–10 minutes.

2. Form dough: Stir in olive oil, then add flour and salt. Mix until a shaggy dough forms.

3. Knead: Turn out onto a floured surface and knead until smooth and elastic, 8–10 minutes. Place in a lightly oiled bowl, cover, and let rise until doubled, 1–1 ½ hours.

4. Shape loaves: Punch down dough and divide in half. Shape into two round loaves and place on a parchment-lined baking sheet. Cover and let rise until puffed, 30–40 minutes.

5. Prepare topping: Brush loaves with beaten egg white. Sprinkle generously with sesame seeds, pressing lightly so they stick.

6. Bake at 375°F (190°C) for 30–35 minutes, until golden brown and hollow-sounding when tapped on the bottom. Cool slightly before slicing.

Servings: 2 round loaves
Prep Time: 20 minutes
(plus 1 ½–2 hours rising)
Cook Time: 35 minutes
Total Time: About 2 ½ hours
Adaptations/Notes: Page 173

The next morning, Nickolas woke early to the sound of roosters crowing, "kikiríkou."

Dazed, he pushed back the covers and ran his fingers through his hair. Realizing Mrs. Kanakis was probably right, he thought it best to use the morning hours studying for his upcoming exams, and wait for the farm families to finish their days' work.

Up to that semester, he had felt confident going into finals week. This one had been hard. He had picked up a couple of additional courses at Compton Junior College. He had been trying to save his parents a little money and stay ahead of the requirements. Seventeen credit hours, classes by day, labs into the evening. Barely enough time left to study.

To complicate matters, the day before his twenty-second birthday, March 10, 1933, the 6.4 magnitude Long Beach earthquake struck. Though the USC campus was untouched, it caused widespread damage at Compton JC. The ancient buildings were quickly declared unsafe and condemned. The small college was closed for weeks. When classes finally resumed, they were at temporary locations, canvas tents, church halls, and community centers. Not only were classes weeks behind schedule, but their revised times and locations didn't fit with Nickolas' schedule at USC.

Behind, and overwhelmed, for the first time, he was concerned about passing. Failure was not an option. He could never do that to his mom and dad. He also knew his college fund was dwindling. Would he be able to re-take the classes he had been forced to drop at Compton JC at USC and still graduate on time? At a much higher tuition rate, no less.

A surge of emotions gripped his body. He was exhausted. He thought of his parents. They must be so tired of being poor. All three of them were working such long hours. Them, in the store, and himself in his studies.

He sat in the guest room at a small writing desk and opened a textbook. From the second floor, he could see the lake far below. A stately Southern Magnolia had grown all the way up to the second floor. He could see its large, creamy white, cup-shaped flowers beside his window. He opened it. A cool breeze brought in the scent of the flowers' rich, lemon-citronella fragrance.

In the 1920s–30s, Lake Elsinore was a glittering resort town of country clubs, mineral baths, a bustling pier, and a yacht club. Considered Southern California's inland Riviera, it was a weekend destination for Hollywood's elite, several of whom owned homes there.

Someday, he thought.

It was the first time he believed they wouldn't struggle forever. The first time he thought maybe the sacrifices they were making would end, and a new life would begin for them.

Those reflections might just have been what Nickolas needed to muster the strength to make it through those last couple of years of dental school. The few days he spent at Mrs. Kanakis' house might have been the break he didn't realize he needed. A time to rest his weary soul. They had hit the ground running in the United States, never pausing. It felt like he'd hardly had time to breathe since he was five years old.

As afternoon approached, he finished up a relatively boring unit on catastrophic neurological events. He committed the symptoms to memory; dilated pupils, slack jaw, prolonged ocular fixation. He closed the textbook and went downstairs. Mrs. Kanakis wished him luck and he set out in the direction of a nearby farm.

What happened next could only be described as a catastrophic neurological event of his own. The most gorgeous woman he had ever seen stepped into view, and Nickolas instantly displayed every symptom the book had warned him about. His higher reasoning was gone. His well-practiced sales pitch dissolved into thin air.

If his professor had been standing there, he could have explained the case on the spot. But there was no need. Nickolas already knew the diagnosis:

love at first sight.

CHAPTER SIX

Mary

Her name was Mary.

She wore what you might imagine a ranch girl would wear. He looked at her as if it was a movie or a book: red and white gingham shirt, work pants, and boots. Hair pulled back neatly in a kerchief, tied in a pretty knot at her forehead. She gathered leaves efficiently, as if the rake were her partner in a dance.

He called her over before realizing he had no idea what to say. He asked her if she knew anything about insurance. She looked confused.

Then, «Μιλάς ελληνικά;», "Do you speak Greek?"

She shook her head.

He could see that her face was beginning to show signs of mistrust. She was about to tell this stranger to get lost when it suddenly occurred to him to drop Mrs. Kanakis' name.

"You're staying with her?" Mary asked.

"Yes," he answered, a little more cheerful than the setting warranted.

She kind of half-smiled.

Mary as a young girl, with her father James and mother Belle, sometime in the early 1920s.

He took that as the tiniest opening to start a small conversation, so he casually mentioned that he was in dental school at USC. He hoped that would impress her. Her eyes met his, but she didn't react.

He didn't ask her out right then and there. He could feel it wasn't the right time. They just talked.

Then he picked up his satchel full of insurance paperwork and moved on to the next farm. She turned and continued to gather leaves.

"Oh, you like dear little Mary," Mrs. Kanakis' later in the day tried to suppress laughter so much that her own eyes started to water.

Women of her stature were careful not to laugh too heartily.

"She's a lovely girl," she continued, collecting herself quickly. "An athlete in high school with a letter jacket full of pins and star patches; volleyball, tennis, basketball, baseball. She made many friends. She was born here in California, you see, so she gets along well with all the girls, the Greek ones and the American ones."

Nickolas felt relieved to hear that she was Greek. His mind began to race. She did, he mused, have the beauty only a Greek goddess could possess, but it was good to have confirmation. His parents would approve. He and Mary had spoken English, yet when he asked if she spoke Greek, he had noticed that she understood him. Maybe he could use their shared heritage as a way of establishing a sort of kinship with her.

Sitting at the table, both Nickolas and Mrs. Kanakis fell silent in thought. Nickolas was simply processing all he heard. Mrs. Kanakis was considering that the young man was in dental school. He would be an incredible catch for a girl like Mary. If she had disapproved, she may have stopped there. Instead, she decided to fill Nickolas in a little more.

TIROPITAKIA
PHYLLO DOUGH CHEESE TRIANGLES

INGREDIENTS

- **1 lb filo dough, room temperature**
- **½ lb feta cheese, crumbled**
- **½ lb cottage cheese**
- **¼ cup grated Romano cheese**
- **2 eggs, lightly beaten**
- **½ cup butter, melted**

HOW TO MAKE IT

1. Preheat oven to 350°F.

2. In a medium bowl, combine feta, cottage cheese, Romano, and eggs. Stir until well blended.

3. Unroll filo and keep sheets covered with a damp towel to prevent drying. Cut filo lengthwise into strips about 3 inches wide.

4. Brush one strip lightly with melted butter. Place 1 tablespoon cheese mixture at one end. Fold the corner over to form a triangle. Continue folding the strip, maintaining the triangle shape, until the end is reached. Brush outside lightly with butter.

5. Place triangles on a greased baking sheet. Bake for 20–25 minutes, or until golden brown.

6. Let cool slightly.

Servings: ~24 triangles
Prep Time: 30 minutes
Cook Time: 20-25 minutes
Total Time: 50–55 minutes
Adaptations/Notes: Page 173

"Mary is the only sister," Mrs. Kanakis continued, "She has three brothers. Two of them have full-time jobs now, and the third just went to Chicago. Tsk. That sweet *koúkla* has had to take on many of the outdoor chores. But that didn't stop her from finishing high school with excellent marks. She just graduated last June. I will say, the young lady can juggle a very demanding schedule. She has learned to be an excellent cook and, with her mother Vasiliki, we call her Belle, keeps an immaculate house." She paused, and then added quietly, "She helps Belle, in so many ways."

Leaving Lake Elsinore too late would mean gas stations along the way would be closed as he passed them. The trip was too long to make on a single tank of gas. It was time to go.

Nickolas was sent off with a wave, a smile, and an invitation to come back anytime. He sensed that Mrs. Kanakis meant it. His presence had cheered her and brought purpose to her in her retirement years. She had someone to cook for.

She handed Nickolas a paper lunch bag. It contained tiropitakia and nectarines from the orchard.

CHAPTER SEVEN
The Road to Another Street

As Nickolas drove, it is entirely possible that, somewhere on that highway that day, there was another vehicle traveling toward Los Angeles, driven by Louis. Like thousands of immigrants during that decade, they left the 4th Ward in East St. Louis and traveled west. They'd heard the weather in California, was sunny, like back home in Greece.

For Louis and Penelope, and their children, the drive west was mostly pleasant. The children sang, then slept peacefully in the car. The weather was temperate. They stopped and picnicked along the way.

The couple welcomed seven children before leaving East St. Louis. Both had come from relatively small families. To them, it was a blessing. Three boys, four girls, and a tomcat named Páki.

When they welcomed their first daughter, they chose a traditional Greek name, Aglaia. They loved the name, but regretted it somewhat. Few outside their circle could pronounce it. They recalled their firstborn, Robert. During his tragically-short life, nobody had trouble pronouncing his name. They coined Aglaia "Helen." From then on, Helen and her siblings were given American-style names, with Greek christening names for tradition.

For two immigrants who didn't know very many names, that sometimes took some comical turns. The second was Catherine. She was named after the silent film actress Catherine Calvert. When Louis suggested the name to a pregnant Penelope, she was delighted.

"It's like Katerina," she smiled, clasping her hands. Ideal. He had found a name that existed in both languages, sort of. The equivalent of St. Catherine in Greek, Katerina is a very common baptismal name. They nicknamed her "Katina," then later, "Tina."

After Catherine, another girl, their third.

They were out of ideas.

ELIOPITA & SKORDALIÁ
ARTISAN GREEK OLIVE BREAD WITH GARLIC DIPPING SAUCE

INGREDIENTS

ELIOPITA ARTISAN GREEK OLIVE BREAD

- 4 cups all-purpose flour
- 1 packet (2 ¼ tsp) active dry yeast
- 1 ½ cups warm water
- 2 tbsp olive oil
- 1 tsp salt
- 1 tsp sugar
- 1 cup pitted Kalamata olives, roughly chopped
- 2 tbsp fresh parsley, chopped

SKORDALIA GARLIC DIPPING SAUCE (NICKOLAS' RECIPE)

- 4 medium potatoes, peeled and cubed
- 6 garlic cloves, crushed
- ½ cup olive oil
- 2 tbsp red wine vinegar
- Salt, to taste

HOW TO MAKE IT

1. In a small bowl, combine yeast, sugar, and warm water. Let sit 10 minutes until foamy.

2. In a large bowl, mix flour and salt. Add yeast mixture and olive oil. Knead until a soft dough forms, about 8–10 minutes.

3. Cover and let rise in a warm place until doubled, about 1 hour.

4. While the dough rises, prepare the

Skordalia. Boil potatoes in salted water until tender, about 15 minutes. Drain and mash until smooth. Crush garlic with a pinch of salt to make a paste. Add garlic paste to potatoes. Beat in olive oil gradually, alternating with vinegar, until fluffy and smooth. Taste and adjust seasoning. Serve at room temperature.

5. Punch down bread dough. Fold in olives, parsley, and oregano. Shape into a round loaf or two smaller loaves.

6. Place on a baking sheet lined with parchment. Cover and let rise again, about 30 minutes.

7. Bake at 375°F for 35–40 minutes, until golden and hollow-sounding when tapped. Cool on a rack before slicing.

Serve with cheeses (feta, kasseri, graviera), and salted or smoked pork cuts. If unavailable, substitute prosciutto, salami or even smoked fish. This can be served charcuterie style, or as a picnic spread.

Servings: 8-10
Prep Time: 30 minutes active (plus 1½ hours rise/rest)
Cook Time: 35–40 minutes
Total Time: 2 hours 30 minutes
Adaptations/Notes: Page 174

ELIOPITA ARTISAN GREEK OLIVE BREAD

SKORDALIA GARLIC DIPPING SAUCE

Weeks went by. They couldn't come up with a name they liked. One morning, while idly monitoring the temperature as he folded condensed milk into chocolate for fudge, Louis thought back. Long ago, back in the old country, he had an uncle. He was tall and red-haired, easy to spot in a crowd.

His business dealings were dubious, and he kept company with an equally questionable French girlfriend.

She was effusively Parisian. The two would stroll the streets of Athens, arm in arm. She, in fur stoles, pierced earrings clinking, had the aroma of sweet perfume and cigarettes. Even if he wore the finest pinstriped, three-piece suit money could buy, she would be the main attraction to all who laid eyes on them. She was not gorgeous, only striking. Hers was the sort of presence that turned heads in the marketplace, though she was not the sort of woman most families would have welcomed at Sunday dinner. Certainly not the sort of woman you named a daughter after. Yet when Louis' third child was born, a girl, he did exactly that. She was Marcelli. To everyone else, simply Marcy.

Next came a boy. That was easy. His name was Nick. If you saw the movie My Big Fat Greek Wedding, you might be nodding now, and laughing. Of course it was Nick. There are always lots of "Nicks."

Nick Louis, after his father.

Then came Harold (Harry), with the middle name Robert, in memory of his deceased older brother.

By that time, the older siblings were school-aged. They helped with the names. Mary Anne, Venita, and seven years later, Dean, a sudden, late-in-life surprise.

1938. UNIVERSITY OF SOUTHERN CALIFORNIA

The class of 1939 at USC was full of women and men, many with foreign-sounding last names. Though none sounded Greek. Nickolas' own classmates in the dental program, if their names are an indication, appear to have all been of Northern European descent.

By 1940, Nickolas Tsetsos had become Dr. Nick Chester.

Throughout his life, Nickolas would identify strongly and proudly with his Greek heritage, but as he made his way through university, he ran with a different crowd, a new set of friends. They were in their junior year.

Monday came, and he had just returned from Lake Elsinore. He spent all day and all night studying. The final was Tuesday. He had a hard time focusing. He could think of nothing but Mary.

That Friday, he nervously entered the classroom. He took a seat next to his friend Woodard.

"Bobby!" he exclaimed, clapping him on the shoulder as he sat. He noticed Woodard looked nervous too.

The graded papers were handed back to them. Nickolas got his first. He aced that final. 100%. He could see Woodard peering over at his paper. He quietly put it on the desk, face down.

There was no reaction when Woodard got his own paper back, so Nicholas didn't ask. None of his business, he figured.

Two more finals to go, and the semester would be over. He crossed campus on foot, heading toward the library. It took a moment for his eyes to adjust inside. He found a desk near the windows, opened his notes, and tried to still his thoughts, which seemed like they were blowing around like feathers. Floating all over the place, that classroom, Lake Elsinore, and everywhere in between.

"Mind if I sit?"

He looked up. Woodard stood there. Tie loosened, face drawn but attempting a smile. Nickolas returned the half-smile.

"Of course," he said.

Woodard lowered himself into the chair across from him. For a while, neither spoke. The only sound was someone typing in a back office.

Finally, Woodard said, "You did well."

Nickolas didn't look up. "I was lucky."

"Lucky," Woodard repeated. "Yeah, maybe." He gave a short laugh, trying sound casual. "Some of us could use a little of that."

Nickolas smiled faintly, hoping to ease the silence.

Woodard's pencil tapped the table once, then again.

He stood, gathering his books. "Yeah, well, don't stay here all night, pal," he added, though it didn't sound like advice.

Mary sells flowers for charity, circa 1942.

Nickolas watched him go, his eyes returning to the notes he couldn't seem to focus on. Nothing seemed easy. He felt restless.

You'll recall that when Louis had arrived in the U.S., his surname was unceremoniously changed to something more easily pronounceable by the immigration officer admitting him into the country. He arrived as Haralambakis, which was recast as Harrison.

The Tsetsos family had a different experience. Upon their own arrival, they must have encountered a more patient border officer. He did transcribe their information correctly and they were able to keep their original last name.

That interaction with Woodard in the library had stayed with him, though he tried to shake it. His friends had surnames like Wells and Wallace. His classmates were Smith and Rice.

He was an American eager to feel a connection to the only home he could remember; California. He grew tired of people stumbling over Tsetsos, and of the instant judgment that followed hearing a name so foreign to their ears.

So Nickolas changed his name on his own.

For Nickolas, his middle name, "Athanasios" became "Thomas," and "Tsetsos" became "Chester."

It was late afternoon in the clinic, the corridors quiet except for the distant hum of a drill. They had just finished assisting on a restorative case. Routine, unremarkable. Nickolas was cleaning the instruments when suddenly he looked up and saw Woodard.

"You've been keeping secrets," Woodard said, a little too lightly.

Nickolas looked up, puzzled. "What do you mean, buddy?"

Woodard gestured toward Wallace and Rice. "The other fellas tell me there's no Tsetsos anymore. Just Chester." He said it slowly, pronouncing every letter.

His tone distracted Nickolas, his hands still in the basin. From some faraway place in his head, he muttered, "I filed the paperwork yesterday. Should be official soon, though I'm not sure it will go through before graduation."

"I see." Woodard smiled faintly, his eyes never looking away from Nickolas, who was not looking back. "Chester suits you. Easy to pronounce."

He leaned against the counter. "You know, people talk. Some say names shouldn't be changed, that it's a kind of disguise. But I suppose everyone's got their reasons."

Nickolas shook excess water off a clean instrument into the sink. "It's simpler," he said. "For patients."

"Of course," Woodard replied, still smiling. "Simpler for patients. Simpler for everyone."

Nickolas stood for a long time, until the sound of the running faucet reminded him to continue washing the instruments.

Nothing seemed simple.

Winter break arrived. he stayed in town for a couple of days to help his father, then headed out to Lake Elsinore. It was his third or fourth trip.

Mrs. Kanakis had grown fond of him. She swung open the door widely, gracefully with a smile. In a song-like voice, she said, "There he is!"

It was late. Too late to see Mary, but he didn't mind. He had three days to spend with her before he'd go home for Christmas. Anyway, an evening with Mrs. Kanakis always passed quickly. She was witty, intelligent and warm. Not to mention that the meals were always exceptional.

He slept well. Whenever he visited, he made sure their time together balanced variety and ease. There would be one dressy dinner out, of course. But just as important, he thought, was giving her the chance to laugh at him trying to mount a horse or watching him panic when a cow looked ready to charge.

On their last night of the visit, she made pastitsio. After setting a generous piece aside for Belle to eat later, she carried the steaming tray outside with oven mitts. She set it on the table, which she had covered with a tablecloth. Then, she carried out a tall, thin bottle and two glasses.

"My brother Andy's homemade wine. He finished this batch just before he left," she said with a shrug and the smallest smirk.

PASTITSIO
KATHY CRANE'S RECIPE FOR GREEK BÉCHAMEL LASAGNA

INGREDIENTS

- **5 lbs ground round or lean ground beef**
- **1 (12 oz) can tomato paste**
- **2 cans water (using the tomato paste can)**
- **1 large onion, finely chopped**
- **Salt and pepper, to taste**
- **Ground cinnamon, to taste**
- **1 package pastitsio pasta**
- **1 stick (½ cup) unsalted butter**
- **1 cup all-purpose flour**
- **1 quart + 2 cups whole milk**
- **10 eggs, lightly beaten**
- **8 ounces grated Romano cheese**

HOW TO MAKE IT

MEAT SAUCE

1. **In a large pot, combine ground beef, tomato paste, water, onion, salt, and pepper.**

2. **Cook over medium heat until the meat is browned, then lower heat and simmer about 1 hour.**

3. **Add cinnamon to taste partway through cooking. Set aside.**

4. **Cook pasta according to package directions until just al dente.**

WHITE SAUCE (BÉCHAMEL)

1. **In a medium saucepan, melt butter over medium heat.**

2. **Stir in flour until smooth. Gradually whisk in milk.**

3. **Cook, stirring constantly, until thickened. Bring just to a boil, then remove from heat.**

4. **Slowly temper beaten eggs into the hot sauce, whisking constantly.**

5. **Season with salt and pepper to taste.**

ASSEMBLY

1. **Preheat oven to 350°F. Butter a large 17" × 12" × 2" baking pan.**

2. **Spread most of the macaroni over the bottom of the pan. Sprinkle generously with Romano cheese.**

3. **Spread meat sauce evenly over pasta, then sprinkle again with Romano.**

4. **Add remaining pasta (about ¼ of the package) over meat layer.**

5. **Pour béchamel sauce evenly over the top, ensuring all pasta is fully covered.**

6. **Bake uncovered for 1½ hours, or until top is golden brown and a thin knife inserted in the center comes out clean.**

7. **Let stand 15 minutes before cutting into squares.**

Servings: 10-12
Prep Time: 45 minutes Cook Time: 1 hour (baking and resting)
Total Time: ~1 hour 45 minutes
Adaptations/Notes: Page 175

They sat together quietly on the back porch, on a large wooden deck with several mature trees shading them from the late afternoon sun. He looked at her. He had not seen her so relaxed. That brought him peace momentarily, but his thoughts turned unexpectedly to Woodard.

He had been wrong that day, when he had thought nothing was simple.

There was one thing: being right where he was, with Mary.

1939. THE WATTS NEIGHBORHOOD OF SOUTH LOS ANGELES

The holiday season came and went, and classes started back up again. Kyrios Thomas had to go downtown to pick up supplies. Nickolas was asked to work in the general store in his place. He didn't mind. It was unlikely it would be too busy. Saturday mornings were never too busy. He'd be able to get some studying in during the downtime.

That morning, the stillness felt heavy, as if the whole town had stayed home. His parents were unusually quiet too. The three of them had driven in without a word. His father stopped the car in the back alley. Nickolas and his mother got out next to the back entrance. The tires crushed the gravel below as he drove away.

Two hours later, Nickolas was deep in his studies. The back door slammed shut, abruptly pulling him away from his textbook. He looked up, dazed. His father had come back in, carrying a wooden crate.

He stood up to help bring in the rest, but his father shook his head.

"No, son, that's all of it for this time," he said.

Nickolas didn't understand. Saturdays were when his father liked to stock up. Unlike on the busy weekdays, Kyria Maria could manage the counter alone. She stood quietly at the register, her hands folded. The clock ticked. From the back room came the faint hum of the cooler.

Then his father spoke again. This time, very softly.

"Son, you won't be going back next term. Hopefully the term after that. God willing."

The words hung in the air. Nickolas didn't look up at first; he thought he must have misheard.

His mother turned away, pulled two Vidalia onions out of a burlap sack, and took a wooden cutting board out of a drawer.

His father cleared his throat. "We just can't make it work right now."

The shop was empty. He could hear nothing but the sound of the clock and, outside, the passing of a car that didn't stop.

That summer, Nickolas would have liked to work long hours in the store to keep his mind off of things, but he wasn't needed. Business was steady enough to keep things afloat, but not so busy that his parents couldn't handle the store with relative ease. Idle time was something he desperately wanted to avoid. His thoughts always drifted to the new term starting without him.

Besides, how could he, in good conscience, propose without any future prospects? A girl like Mary deserved a steady man.

On one such afternoon, unneeded inside, he decided to go out back to have a cigarette. Standing outside in the alley, he tried his best to come up with a plan. He had already sold insurance to anyone he knew who would buy.

His father had spoken for months about opening up a second location. But he had always said that would have to wait until Nickolas was finished with school.

If they didn't have the money for his tuition, another store would be out of the question. Then it came to him. Another store would be impossible, but another *location* might not.

Excitedly, Nickolas poked his head inside. "I'll be back later," he called to his mother. She nodded, and he left.

He half-walked, half-jogged all the way home. When he finally got there, he was sweaty, but he didn't go inside. Instead, he opened the garage, grabbed some tools and headed to the backyard, where there was a pile of wood.

When he was finished, he found an old can of yellow paint, and he took apart his childhood bicycle so that he could use the wheels.

He had built a food cart. If they couldn't open another store, he'd sell his parents goods on busy street corners and outside sporting events. Hell, he thought, remembering that school would be starting back up in the fall without him, I have nothing better to do.

He had wanted to paint *Chester's Cuisine* on the side of the cart. But his parents still considered him a Tsetsos. Nickolas was their only child. He hadn't told them.

So, he went with *Delicious Homemade Meals on the Go.*

Just then, his father pulled the car into the driveway. His parents reacted with marvel. But their eyes gave them away. With all that talent and creativity, how regrettable that he would not be able to continue his education. It had been their one dream.

Every day, Nickolas would scan the newspaper for major local events. He would work outside ball games, concerts, anything that would draw a crowd. During the week, he'd wheel the cart alongside local office buildings, construction sites, anywhere he thought there would be hungry people in need of a good meal on the go.

It wasn't exactly a get-rich-quick scheme, but it brought in more than enough cash to make it well worth the effort. At lunchtime, he'd have a long line, but it was short-lived. A lot of prep and cleanup for an hour of actual business. It was useless to stay around past 1:00 or 1:30. Once the rush was over, there was no more money to be made.

After some trial and error, he found big, hungry lunch crowds at the edge of the Nickel district, right along the 6th Street Corridor between Main and Los Angeles Streets. There were several construction sites in the area.

At first, the pack of burly, foul-mouthed workers was intimidating. They jokingly referred to him as "the Greek goddess," as they elbowed one another's ribs and laughed. But his food was "damn good," they said. He started to get a following.

Kyria Maria's homemade soup was his best-seller. For ten cents, he'd give you a bowl and a thick slice of bread, freshly baked that morning. Some of the bigger men would order two portions.

Patrons could bring their own tin bowls. If they didn't have one, Nickolas would ladle the soup into an enamelware one of his own, and they'd bring it back when they were finished.

Except once.

One of the construction workers who had never quite warmed up to him ordered soup and took off with Nickolas' bowl. Nickolas assumed he would bring it back the next day, but he didn't.

Nickolas noticed him in line, empty-handed.

He gave the customer he was serving his change, cut a thick slice of bread, placed it beside the bowl, thanked him, and watched him walk off before turning to the man without a bowl.

The man met his gaze squarely, voice loud and sure.

"Soup. Need a bowl."

"Sorry, pal," Nickolas said evenly, "you'll need to bring me back my bowl. I can wash it and refill it for you. Won't take but a second."

"Don't worry about it," the man said, voice thick with challenge.

Nickolas was stunned when the man took a tiny pocket knife out and drew the little blade. Their eyes locked. While they were staring at each other, the man slid his hand down and took the entire loaf of bread sitting on the cart between them.

Then, he ran off.

The customer next in line saw the whole thing. He shouted to Nickolas, "Go on! I'll watch the stand!"

Nickolas grabbed the knife he had been using to cut the bread and took off after the thief. He had run track in high school, so he caught up with him easily and kicked the back of his knees. The man fell to the ground. Nickolas stood over him, holding the knife.

The bread was useless at that point, but things were different after that.

"You gotta watch that Neecko,' a customer said the next day, shaking his head. 'He's got a bigger knife than that other fella.'

The group of workers with him roared with laughter. From then on, when Nickolas needed a wall fixed, a porch mended, or a new door hung, he never paid more than a handshake, and maybe a few bowls of soup.

Summer began to draw to a close. He tried his best not to think of USC. Not only that, he still hadn't had the courage to tell his parents about the name change. He felt heavy inside.

He wasn't the least bit concerned if they directed some angry feelings toward him. That, he could manage. It was their disappointment he dreaded. He was going to need to come clean.

In the late afternoons, after being on his feet all day, it was always the hardest to push the cart back up through the gravel alleyway, into the rear entrance of the store. Finally, hot and exhausted, he shoved it inside with a final push and started gathering the things he would need to clean it and prepare it for the next day.

Hearing him come in, his parents both walked in back. He looked up, surprised. His father managed to look somber, but his mother was smirking.

"Son," Kyrios Thomas said, trying to sound serious, "put the cart away. It will be good to use next summer. For now, you won't be needing it anymore. You will register for the fall semester tomorrow."

Neither of them could keep a straight face any longer. Both laughed, releasing happy energy into the room. Nickolas was shocked. Several seconds went by before he was able to join in. Then, tears of pure relief. It was the first time in his life he could ever remember being so happy that he cried. He would be going back to school after all.

It took them a minute or two to collect themselves, then his father continued, somber once again,

"Ahem, will you be registering as Tsetsos, or Chester, Son?"

He hadn't told them, but they had found out anyway. It probably didn't take long for them to overhear others using "Chester," and even the many iterations of Nicholas: "Neecko," "Nick," "Nicky."

Kyria Maria stared at the floor. Nickolas didn't know if she was anticipating the worst, or trying to keep a straight face. He froze.

GÁMOKOULOURA
WEDDING BREAD

INGREDIENTS

- 2 cups warm water (110°F)

- 2 tsp active dry yeast

- 1 Tbsp sugar

- 6–7 cups all-purpose flour, divided

- 1 tsp salt

- ½ cup olive oil

- ½ cup honey

- 2 large eggs

- 1 Tbsp anise seeds (optional)

- ½ cup sesame seeds, for topping

HOW TO MAKE IT

1. In a large bowl, combine warm water, yeast, and sugar. Let sit until foamy, about 10 minutes.

2. Stir in 3 cups of the flour, salt, olive oil, honey, eggs, and anise seeds (if using). Mix until smooth.

3. Gradually add remaining flour, ½ cup at a time, until dough is soft but not sticky.

4. Knead on a floured surface for 8–10 minutes, or until elastic.

5. Place dough in an oiled bowl, cover, and let rise until doubled, about 1½–2 hours.

6. Punch down and shape into a large round or braided ring. Transfer to a parchment-lined baking sheet.

7. Brush with water and sprinkle generously with sesame seeds. Cover and let rise again, about 45 minutes.

8. Preheat oven to 350°F. Bake bread 35–45 minutes, or until golden brown and hollow-sounding when tapped.

9. Cool on a rack before serving.

Traditionally, coins or small crosses were sometimes tucked into the dough before baking, symbolizing prosperity and blessing. The bread was set at the center of the wedding table and shared among family and guests.

Prep Time: 30 minutes active (mixing, kneading, shaping)
Rise Time: 2½–3 hours total (first and second rise)
Cook Time: 35–45 minutes
Total Time: ~3½–4 hours
Adaptations/Notes: Page 175

His father's voice broke the silence.

"Τὸ ὄνομα οὐσίαν οὐ ποιεῖ," ("The name does not make the essence,) he bellowed, his belly shaking in laughter.

"Plato said so," he continued, apparently quite amused.

And so it was Mr. Chester who re-registered in school. With his future secure once again, he took the first opportunity to make the trip to Lake Elsinore and proposed to Mary. She was barely fluent in Greek, but he had his parents' blessing, which was all that mattered to him. When Nickolas tried to voice his appreciation for their openess on that subject, they told him not to "be silly."

Mrs. Kanakis checked with her neighbor Belle whenever she saw her outside. Both women waited, on edge, for Mary to make up her mind.

The truth is, when he had asked, she wasn't sure what her answer would be. After a day or two of thinking it over, she said yes.

CHAPTER EIGHT
Headlines

The Japanese had already attacked Pearl Harbor. Weddings had a different tone with the war as a constant backdrop. Some would say more positive. Many would flip straight to the announcement page of the newspaper, eager for any joyful news, and tired of endless war coverage.

Both Mary and Nickolas had a sharp eye for style. Nickolas had waited to marry until he was finished with dental school. In the 1940s, that meant he was marrying later than most. Still, it suited him just fine.

He had just finished school but hadn't opened his own practice yet; the extra year or two allowed him to save.

At the time, films like MGM Studios' 1941 blockbuster "Ziegfeld Girl" were showcases of panache, with over-the-top mirrored furniture, sweeping staircases, luxurious bedrooms; It was Hollywood Regency fantasy at full throttle. After Art Deco and its streamlined modernism had dominated for years, glamour was back in.

The wedding of Doctor and Mrs. Chester, April 19, 1942.

Mary and her mother Belle planned meticulously, and created true elegance on a budget. The wedding was beautiful. It took place in Hollywood, in 1942.

It wasn't big, but it was bespoke. All of the touches had Mary's chic, breezy signature. Mary herself radiated with loveliness that, in Nickolas' eye, could rival any starlet at the time.

Nickolas walked down the aisle hand in hand with his new bride.

Doctor and Mrs. Chester.

Soon, he started doing well in his dental practice. Although World War II was in full swing, dentistry is always needed. They bought a house and a car, and had their first child, a son. He was named Thomas, after Nickolas' father.

When they started to became too old to care for themselves, Kyrios Thomas and Kyria Maria moved in with them. Years later, Mary said they were a pleasure to have around, very helpful with the children. In fact, she said, with her in-laws living in her home, her Greek improved quite a bit.

The couple became active in their church community, helping to establish the landmark St. Sophia Cathedral in Los Angeles. For a time, Nickolas served as president of the congregation, which had grown into one of the largest in the city. They were deeply charitable, giving generously of their time and resources.

Their circle of friends was as eager as they were to experience all the city had to offer. The Biltmore Hotel, the Casbah on Figueroa, the Moulin Rouge on Sunset, and the Hollywood Bar of Music on Beverly Boulevard.

Nickolas had a smooth, baritone singing voice. That, combined with his expressive personality made him a perfect fit for the neighborhood barbershop quartet and for lead roles in local plays.

A couple of months after their wedding, the musical motion picture "Yankee Doodle Dandy" with James Cagney made its debut in theaters.

Nickolas was obsessed with the songs, and would belt them out at home anytime they bubbled up to the surface inside him, which was often.

Even then, he realized they were good years. He felt he had everything he had ever wanted.

It had been a hot summer, but the weather was finally cooling. Kyria Maria decided to take advantage of the beautiful afternoon. She seated herself on a chair on the front porch of her son and daughter-in-law's home, where she was now living. She watched

CLOTHES DO MAKE A BARBERSHOP QUARTET, as this foursome proved to the Gay Nineties audience Saturday night at the Morningside Park Woman's Club dinner dance at Mayflower Ballroom. In action for their part in the Diamond Horseshoe Revue are, (kneeling left), Gage Chrysler, Walt Marrin; standing, Nicholas Chester, Roland Ingraham. (Hanson Williams photo)

A newspaper clipping featuring Nickolas with his barbershop quartet, complete with striped suits, bowties, straw hats and fake moustaches. One of the countless local productions, radio shows, and plays he appeared in.

her grandson, Tommy, toddle around on grass shaded by a large Camphor tree. He had a small, metal toy submarine in his outstretched hand and was running in unsteady circles making gurgling sounds.

The newsboy rode by and threw that evening's copy of the paper close to where Kyria Maria was sitting. They waved at one another, and he rode on. She rose, with some difficulty, and collected the paper. She didn't know how to read in English, but she liked to look at it anyway.

Nickolas pulled the car into the driveway. He was home from work. He walked across the yard, scooped up Tommy in his arms, and the boy giggled. Carrying him, he continued toward the front porch. He was about to give his mother a kiss on the cheek when he noticed the headline on the paper she was holding: Draft Boards to Remove Nearly All Deferments as Quotas Tighten.

Nickolas' body went cold. He knew what it meant. The U.S. wasn't just fighting in Europe anymore. Now, they were involved in what they were calling a "two front war," both in Europe and in the South Pacific. The demand for servicemen had nearly doubled.

A single headline could alter a man's fate, and this one had just sentenced him.

He felt dizzy. His hands still ached from a full day's worth of dental work. He just stood there, short of breath.

Marriage and fatherhood were supposed to keep him safe, and they had, up to that point. In April of that same year, Selective Service had reclassified men, tightening deferments. By August 1942, being married alone was no longer enough to avoid the draft. But Nickolas still had fatherhood to protect him, he reasoned. Plus, he was 31. Although they were drafting up to age 35, he had hoped he was getting too old.

There on his own front porch, those hopes disappeared in an instant. He scanned the article. By mid to late 1942, the manpower need was so great that even many men with one dependent child were losing their deferments. Upon reading that, Nickolas knew immediately that he would be one of the first to go. Dental professionals like himself were actually targeted by the draft and commissions. Even if you were married with a child, your skill set put you at the front of the line for specialized service.

At dinner, Nickolas' voice shook as he explained to his wife and parents that the U.S. armed forces were no longer looking at rings on fingers. They were looking at empty bunks. By summer, marriage and children were no shield, and Nickolas' profession put him squarely in their sights.

It wasn't long before the draft letter arrived, but the days leading up to it made the thirty steps out to the mailbox pure hell. No matter which family member fetched the mail.

CHAPTER NINE

The Bitterness of Combat

1942. EAST ST. LOUIS, ILLINOIS

Both Nick and Harry were drafted. Dean was still just a boy, too young to serve.

Penelope had managed to stay strong, or at least give her husband that impression, when Nick got his draft letter. But when the second set of papers arrived, this time for Harry, it was more than she could bear. She felt sorry for Louis when he walked in and saw her with Harry at the kitchen table. She wished he hadn't seen her crumpled in fear and grief, slouched, head in hands. She was just about to get up to get Harry a handkerchief, too. By seconds, she missed shielding her husband from the sight of their son's first and only tears he would shed in front of his father.

Lying on the white, waxed lace tablecloth was the letter. Harry bolted up and sprinted out of the room. Down the hallway, his bedroom door slammed.

Louis sat down next to her.

Through her sobs, it was difficult for her to get words out. But it was wartime. Louis already knew. This was described later to me by their third son, Dean, as a turning point for the couple. All of their children had been born in the United States.

This was when they both realized they were home.

Louis held Penelope's trembling hand. «Μη κλαις, Πένη μου...»

"Don't cry, my Peni," he said, although tears were forming in his own eyes. "These are very bad men we fight against. They must be stopped. God willing our sons will return, but now we must protect our *patrída* (homeland)."

And just like that, Penelope said, they were Americans for life.

She'd say, when you're an immigrant, that realization is a discovery that hits you one day. The scales tip, and suddenly your new country is more familiar to you than the old world from whence you came. Finally, without warning, it's "home."

It was, as always, for better or for worse. In Penelope and Louis' case, they had lost their firstborn, Robert, as a baby, and were sending two more of their boys off to war.

During World War II, American families displayed service flags (also called Blue Star Banners) in their windows. A blue star meant a family member was serving in the military. Penelope hung two blue stars in the front window.

If that family member died in service, the blue star was changed to a gold star.

In their neighborhood, Penelope only saw one.

Walking home from a shopping trip one day, she spotted it, freshly hung, in the window of a house up the street from hers. A gold star. She made her way home, stunned.

The next day, she gathered her own freshly-made Kourabiedes and walked to Louis' candy store. Louis was busy behind the counter, but he gave her a quick wink. She made her way past the wooden cases, into the back, where the packing area was. There, she picked a thick, white candy box.

Just the right size for the Kourabiedes, with some room to spare. She used foil cups, and added some of Louis' most popular candies from the store inventory.

Louis came in back to say a quick hello. He already knew of his wife's planned visit to Mrs. Miller's house. He saw the box and laughed.

"Kariokes, kourabiedes" he chuckled idly, "for a funeral."

Penelope picked up on Louis' quiet humor. Both sweets were usually used as name-day treats and on other festive occasions. Both knew Mrs. Miller wouldn't know the difference. Anyway, they were among the most delicious.

They laughed genuinely at the irony, and Louis returned to the front of the store. When she had reached for the Kariokes, it had just felt right. Penelope felt extra empathy in handing over a piece of her own history. She was filling the box with care.

Mrs. Miller might even sense that there was something special besides sugar and flour in that package.

Besides, she instinctively knew Mrs. Miller would like them.

When she was happy with the neat rows of sweets, she tied it with silky ribbon in black. Nothing that looked festive would do. Placing it gently in her basket, she quietly slipped out of the back, with just a small wave to her husband, who was already serving new customers.

KARIOKES
LOUIS' NO-BAKE RECIPE FOR CHOCOLATE-WALNUT SWEETS

INGREDIENTS

- 2 cups walnuts, finely chopped

- ½ cup graham cracker or biscuit crumbs (or finely crushed petit beurre cookies)

- ½ cup powdered sugar

- 2 Tbsp cocoa powder

- ¼ cup brandy or sweet wine

- ½ cup plant-based butter, melted and cooled slightly

- 12 oz good-quality dark chocolate (60–70% cocoa), chopped

HOW TO MAKE IT

1. In a mixing bowl, combine walnuts, cookie crumbs, powdered sugar, and cocoa powder.

2. Stir in brandy (or wine) and melted butter until mixture holds together like a thick paste.

3. Shape mixture into small oval or teardrop patties, about 2 inches long. Place on a parchment-lined tray and refrigerate 30 minutes to firm up.

4. Melt chocolate gently in a heatproof bowl set over a pan of simmering water (double boiler method), stirring until smooth.

5. Dip each walnut patty in the melted chocolate, using a fork to coat evenly. Place on parchment paper to set.

6. Chill briefly to harden the chocolate, but serve at room temperature for best flavor.

Kariokes are typically festive, name-day treats. Penelope recognized Mrs. Miller wouldn't know the difference, and she wanted the best for her.

Servings: 20–24 pieces
Prep Time: 30 minutes
Chill Time: 30 minutes
Cook Time: 0 (no-bake, except for melting chocolate)
Total Time: ~1 hour
Adaptations/Notes: Page 176

She walked to the front of the store. She could already feel the chill outside, so she turned and set the box on one of the small tables nearest the door and put on her hat, then her coat.

With her back to them, she heard two women walk in. They were in the midst of a lively gossip.

"For a Levantine family, they're actually not bad people, I'll admit. Of course I'd shop elsewhere if I could, but his are the best we can get around here."

"Oh, yes," the other one agreed. "I was quite taken aback when they moved into the neighborhood, but I was just telling Ronald the other day that it's helpful we have their store here. There just isn't anything else like it around. I'm not sure he agrees, but I got the impression he doesn't mind if I shop here. He has a sweet tooth, you know."

The first woman laughed, with a quick toss backward of her head. Then, they greeted Louis as if they were the best of friends. He, in turn, greeted them warmly.

Penelope felt cold inside, and it wasn't due to the weather. Was this a sign? Would Mrs. Miller find her visit odd? If she did, would Penelope even know it? Or, would she feign graciousness like these two.

She looked at them. She had never seen these women. Louis appeared to have seen them before. If their appearances were anything to judge by, they looked solidly lower-middle class. They used "Levantine" instead of a more outright slur to make themselves sound more educated, as if they were above crude discrimination from one Caucasian to another, albeit with different skin tone. They both avoided her gaze.

Back outside, she felt a single freezing tear fall. She wiped it away as she walked quickly, clutching the package.

She was irritated. Why would those two act that way? She decided to dismiss it, otherwise she might run out of courage and turn back.

Then, her thoughts turned to Mrs. Miller, and her slain son. What a useless loss of life! May God punish those who do these terrible things to innocent boys, people's sons. They should become husbands and fathers, not lie in graves.

Then, fear for her own boys. It had been a week or so since she had received a letter. They were fine then, but it was anyone's guess where they were today.

Finally, as she approached the home, she felt a wave of nervousness. It's always a little awkward to talk to those in mourning. Would her visit be appreciated? She would never know if Mrs. Miller was silently judging her while greeting her graciously

She tried to come to her senses. Mrs. Miller had always waved and smiled. She wasn't at all like the two catty women she had seen at the store. Then again, Penelope's English wasn't perfect. Her mind ran. What would she say?

KOURABIEDES
THE BITE-SIZED BUTTER PASTRY THAT GAVE THIS BOOK ITS NAME

INGREDIENTS

- 1 lb (450 g) unsalted, plant-based butter, softened

- 1 tbsp granulated sugar

- 2 egg yolks

- 2 tbsp whiskey

- 1½ tsp vanilla extract

- 1 tsp baking powder

- 4½ cups sifted all-purpose flour (approximate)

- Whole cloves (for garnish)

- Powdered sugar (for dusting)

- Small, pleated paper candy cups (for serving)

HOW TO MAKE IT

1. Preheat oven to 350°F (175°C). Line baking sheets with parchment paper.

2. Cream the butter in a large bowl until smooth and fluffy. Add sugar and beat until light.

3. Add the egg yolks, whiskey, and vanilla, beating until incorporated.

4. In a separate bowl, sift together the baking powder and flour. Gradually add to the butter mixture, using only as much flour as needed for a soft, pliable dough.

5. Form small balls of dough and gently pinch the tops with four fingers to shape. Insert a whole clove in the top of each cookie.

6. Arrange cookies on prepared sheets and bake for 35–40 minutes, or until the bottoms are lightly golden.

7. While still warm, sprinkle powdered sugar over a clean baking sheet. Place hot cookies on top, then sift more powdered sugar generously over them.

8. When completely cool, remove cloves and transfer each cookie to a small, pleated paper candy cup for serving.

Watch closely while baking to avoid under- or overcooking. The whiskey deepens both flavor and aroma, though brandy or ouzo may be used instead. Traditionally, these cookies are served at Christmas and weddings, symbolizing joy and purity. They are also the namesake of this book; kourabiedes being the plural form of kourabies.

Servings: About 3 dozen cookies
Prep Time: 20 minutes
Cook Time: 40 minutes total
Total Time: 1 hour
Adaptations/Notes: Page 176

Back home, a visit like this would have been easy.

She closed her eyes and knocked. It had started to drizzle.

After endless seconds, Mrs. Miller came to the door. Her face was bare. Her eyes were swollen and red.

The two women looked at each other. Penelope lowered her head and half-smiled, "a little something for you," she said, extending the box toward her neighbor. "Mrs. Miller, I am so sorry for your loss."

She had rehearsed it a thousand times. She had said it better sometimes when she was alone, but she didn't think her English sounded too bad.

Mrs. Miller looked up at her. After a pause, she began to cry uncontrollably. She mumbled that she was sorry, and leaned against the front door, gesturing for Penelope to come in, while she held a crumpled tissue to her face.

They sat down on the sofa against the front window, just below the gold star banner. Mrs. Miller sniffed and set the package of sweets down beside her. Neither said anything.

Penelope studied her; she stared at the floor and was trembling. As a mother of sons fighting in the war herself, Penelope knew what to do. She laid her hand gently on top of Mrs. Miller's, not squeezing, just resting.

There was no need to worry about finding words in English to comfort her neighbor after all. For this, there were no words. In any language.

It took five full minutes before Mrs. Miller could speak. When she did, her unsteady voice carried grief and disappointment that pierced Penelope's heart.

"You..." she sniffled, "you, um, were," she continued, gulped then continued louder, as if she needed to force the words out. Then, in the clearest tone she could muster,

"You are the only one who came after I hung the star."

It turned out the others on the street had been afraid to approach Mrs. Miller. Sometimes, in her darkest moments, she wondered if anyone had even noticed the gold star, representing that her child was now just a war casualty. Through new tears, she said hadn't had a single visit since the memorial service. Penelope had been the sole neighbor who had made such a gesture.

She walked back home quietly, her throat still tight with emotion. The visit hadn't been easy, yet she couldn't help thinking how cowardly everyone else had been toward this poor woman. Instead of being given comfort she deserved, Mrs. Miller had been sitting in her house alone with her immeasurable grief.

She vowed to herself, the next time she saw those two women in Louis' candy store, she would not look away."

CHAPTER TEN

War's Unknown Predestination

To be drafted is to gamble with survival. Those who stay behind, and those who return home, find no victory in their luck. Families are broken, futures rewritten, and the shadow falls on everyone, enemy or friend. It is a lottery where no ticket is a winning one, only different shades of loss.

In a sense, Nickolas was fortunate during those war years. His schooling benefited him. He wasn't placed on the front lines. Instead, he served as a dental officer on large Navy ships. Probably the worst thing he saw were some very horrific teeth. He made lifelong friends. Twice he was granted leave, long enough to see his family. Although he didn't realize it at the time, on one of those visits home he and Mary conceived his second child, a girl.

During World War II, both chocolate and cigarettes were standard parts of U.S. military rations. They were small comforts, light to carry, handed out by the millions through the Red Cross, the USO, and military supply lines. Every K-ration and C-ration included a tiny pack of cigarettes (usually 4 per meal box). They were donated by big companies like Lucky Strike, Camel, Chesterfield, and Old Gold, which also ran patriotic advertising campaigns. The Hershey Company developed the infamous Hershey's D-Ration (a high-calorie, heat-resistant chocolate bar) specifically for the U.S. Army. By all accounts, it tasted terrible. The soldiers used to joke that the bars were "Hitler's Secret Weapon," meaning they were so bad that they must have been supplied by the enemy. Nickolas agreed. He would trade them to anyone who didn't smoke, in exchange for their cigarettes.

Nick and Harry would have received Hershey's Tropical Bar. They were both stationed in the South Pacific, and that bar was designed for hotter climates. It was the D-Ration, only drier and slightly more salty. There was hardly a hint of chocolate. It was hard to believe there could be something worse than the original, but one taste was convincing enough.

Nick Harrison entered as a warrant officer at age 31. His civil engineering background was a big help to their wartime efforts. He was wanted for his expertise. He wasn't required to be in combat. Wartime, of course is difficult, regardless. Both Nick Harrison and Nickolas Chester would have faced challenges.

But things were much worse for Harry.

He was just 19 when he received his draft letter in 1943. Unlike his much older brother, he had barely started college. Unlike Nickolas Chester, he was single, not yet married.

He was sent to the front lines.

His unit had been sent to scout a new position in a location near Bougainville that command wanted them to occupy. They spread out to search the ground. Before long, Harry found himself alone. Even if he found a place in the shade to stand and survey the surroundings, the pressure of the intense humidity pressing against his entire body almost made him feel like he was under water. He was so accustomed to the stale stench of wet, rotting leaves that he had learned to ignore it. Still it was always there. Mud sucked at his boots with every step, making a sound as he trod along.

That was when he saw them. A column of enemy soldiers, rifles slung, boots striking the dirt in unison. They were moving straight toward him.

Harry dropped back into the brush. Branches pressed hard into his sweaty back. The sting of thorns bore into his arms, and burned, but he did not move. The enemy soldiers passed with just a shrub separating them, their voices low, weapons clattering, footsteps mere feet away.

He did not breathe. He did not dare. A single shift of weight, a snap of a twig beneath him, and it would have been over.

He waited until he could hear nothing but the sound of insects buzzing. Stepping out of that bush was terrifying. What if they had gathered nearby, and stopped? He questioned his own judgment.

The German occupation of Athens was announced on October 12, 1944. Greeks all over the world took to the streets and celebrated when the Nazi occupiers lowered their swastika flag from the Acropolis.

The war was finally ending.

After years of darkness, at last, there was some optimistic news to spread. The soldiers sent letters assuring their loved ones that they would be home soon.

Instead, the months dragged on.

Harry was so tired when he heard about Germany's overall unconditional surrender on May 8, 1945. It was official. Once again, they hoped they might finally be going home.

But the war was still raging in the Pacific. Their initial wave of relief and joy shifted quickly to disappointment when official orders made clear that large numbers would be redeployed to Asia or kept in occupation duty. The U.S. was preparing for the invasion of Japan (Operation Downfall), which was expected to be even bloodier than the war fought in Europe. The phrase "redeployment, not demobilization" was used a lot. It was a bitter distinction. It meant something only to the military. Nothing to a soldier.

So both Harry and Nick stayed right where they were. Their only respite was a letter, or maybe an occasional small tin of paximádia that Penelope had lovingly sent. The Greek biscotti were the ideal care package, strong enough to withstand the shipment a continent away. They would dip them in their morning instant coffee. They could last weeks, even months, in a tin.

One morning, in the officer's dining hall, a stocky, muscular man behind him in line watched intently as Nick unwrapped two paximádia and placed them on his meal tray beside a cup of watery coffee. Feeling the man's stare, Nick looked up at him.

Surprisingly, his face was full of fondness.

"Are those Greek?" he asked. He spoke in a thick Greek accent. He introduced himself as a liaison officer, John. He explained he came from the Peloponnese. A casual "What village?" opened the door.

"Dad's from Messene, mother was born in Koroni," Nick said.

The man laughs softly. "Ah, Koroni. Then you must know the Vrachonis family. The son made quite a name for himself."

"So I've heard," Nick answers carefully. He didn't know. He had no idea.

The man's tone turned dry. "Well, he's made another one now."

PAXIMÁDIA
GREEK BISCOTTI

INGREDIENTS

- 1 cup unsalted, plant-based butter, softened
- 1 cup granulated sugar
- 4 large eggs
- 1 tsp vanilla extract
- 1 tsp almond extract (optional, traditional variation)
- Zest of 1 orange
- 4 cups all-purpose flour
- 2 tsp baking powder
- ½ tsp ground cinnamon
- ½ tsp ground cloves
- ½ tsp salt
- 1 cup chopped almonds or walnuts (optional)

HOW TO MAKE IT

1. Preheat oven to 350°F (175°C). Lightly grease two baking sheets or line with parchment paper.

2. In a large bowl, cream butter and sugar until light and fluffy. Beat in eggs one at a time, then add vanilla, almond extract, and orange zest.

3. In a separate bowl, sift together flour, baking powder, cinnamon, cloves, and salt. Gradually add dry ingredients to the wet mixture, stirring until a soft dough forms. Fold in nuts if using.

4. Divide dough in half and shape each portion into a log about 12 inches long and 3 inches wide. Place on prepared sheets.

5. Bake for 25–30 minutes, or until lightly golden and firm to the touch. Remove from oven and cool for 10 minutes.

6. Lower oven temperature to 300°F (150°C). Slice logs diagonally into ½-inch pieces. Lay slices cut side down on baking sheets.

7. Bake again for 12–15 minutes per side, until crisp and golden. Cool completely before storing.

8. Biscotti-like pastries are too crisp to bite. They are meant to dip in coffee or hot chocolate to soften, bite by bite, before enjoying.

For a more rustic Greek flavor, substitute part of the flour with whole-wheat or barley flour.

Store in an airtight container; they keep beautifully for weeks.

Servings: 24–30 biscotti
Prep Time: 20 minutes
Chill Time: 10 minutes (cooling between bakes)
Cook Time: 55–60 minutes total
Total Time: ~1 hour 30 minutes
Adaptations/Notes: Page 177

May 28, 1944
Espiritu Santo, New Hebrides, South Pacific

Dear Mother and Father,

I am in good health, and I hope you are too. Please write back and tell me if you have had any letters from Harry. I pray every day that he is doing fine. I got word that his unit did see some casualties, but last I heard, Harry was unhurt. Communication is possible sometimes. Other days, systems are not functioning.

I've been reassigned, attached to a Navy construction unit under the Corps of Engineers.

I happened to meet a Greek officer this week, stationed nearby for liaison work. When he learned my family was from Koroni, he smiled and said it's a small world. Then he asked if I knew the Vrachonis family.

Do either of you know anyone by that name? I wrote it down so I could ask you about it.

He shared a bit of village gossip with me. There was a man, he was from a well-to-do family. He got a post working in the Prefecture Office in Kalamata. I'm told, he was hired in party by his father's "war hero" reputation. But the man I met said he didn't think the man was a real war hero. He said nobody in Koroni believed that.

At any rate, he married a woman from a wealthy family in Kalamata and settled there. I guess she was a real fancy one, of Venetian descent. Rumor has it, even on his good, government salary, he couldn't maintain the lifestyle she expected. A lot of money went missing from the coffers. He's in jail now, lost everything. They say he'll face trial once the war is over.

It's strange, hearing names from home this far away. I thought you'd want to know.

Your loving son,

Nick

Penelope sat at the kitchen table, reading her son's words. She could hardly wait to show it to Louis when he came home.

She re-read it, quietly mouthing the name.

"Vrachonis."

The air seemed so still.

She hadn't thought of them in years.

For a moment, she was back in Koroni, hearing their boasts in her father's parlor, the false swagger.

She folded the letter slowly and pressed it against her heart. "God sees all," she whispered.

Out at sea, it took longer for word of Germany's surrender to reach Nickolas. He was lying on the hard mattress in his cramped, metal bunk when it was announced over the ship's loudspeaker.

In his case, as with all Navy medical personnel, that news would have meant nothing to his deployment. The Navy was still stretched across the Pacific.

None of them would be going home after all.

Weighing heavily on him was the possibility that he would not be home in time for the birth of his daughter.

SEPTEMBER 2, 1945. TOKYO BAY

None of them knew it then, but Japan would be the real endpoint for the soldiers. From the perspective of those far from home, the transition from total war to total surrender happened astonishingly fast. August was bloody and intense. Then suddenly it was over.

They all crowded around the radio, listening to the broadcast crackle out a barely audile message: the Japanese delegation had boarded the USS Missouri. Foreign Minister Mamoru Shigemitsu and General Yoshijirō Umezu had signed the surrender documents.

For quite a while after Nick and Harry were sent home, Nickolas was still at sea. He had been given one final assignment as a dental officer on the Admiral C. F. Hughes. The ship's task was to round up servicemen from scattered posts around the globe and bring them home. Many mouths were in need of care, with cavities and cleanings neglected for years. In his chair sat prisoners of war newly freed and soldiers on their last voyage before returning to civilian life. It was a surreal mix. There was so much trauma and exhaustion, yet an unmistakable current of joy ran through everyone on board as men anticipated seeing

October, 1944: Nazi soldiers lower the swastika flag at the Parthenon. The Germans had surrendered under Allied pressure, and finally left Greece.

their loved ones again, this time for good. He hardly wanted to put gauze in their mouths, rendering them temporarily speechless. Their stories were too interesting to miss.

Below deck at night, Nickolas lay in his cot, listening to the engines hum and thinking of Mary. She was home, about to give birth to their second child. He didn't know exactly what he felt: grateful, restless, suspended between worlds. He didn't quite fit into either group. The waiting, the same long waiting the whole world had endured for the horror to end, provided they got out alive, was the hardest part for him in those final days.

Harry returned cam home uninjured. On the outside, anyway. Internally, he struggled for a while.

His older brother Nick had come home to his wife and started a family. His first born was a girl, making Louis and Penelope grandparents for the first time. His second, a boy. Their names? Penelope and Louis, of course. The younger ones were known as Penny and Lew.

Harry would marry later and have a family of his own.

They were home. There was celebration after celebration, but the memories would stay with Penelope. Every parent, every wife, who had prayed for a blue star to

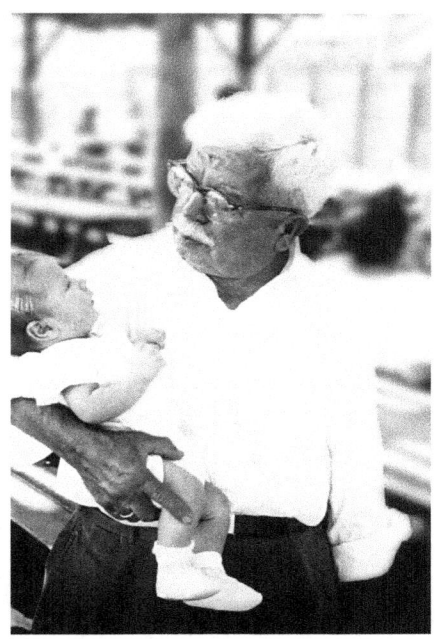

Louis Harrison holding his namesake, baby Louis (Lew) Harrison, his son Nick's second born, 1953.

stay blue now learned how to live with ghosts that would never quite leave.

PSARI PLAKI
BAKED BRANZINO WITH TOMATO AND ONION

INGREDIENTS

- 2 lbs wild-caught branzino (or most any other firm whitefish fillet)

- 4 large onions, thinly sliced

- 3 cloves garlic, minced

- 4 ripe tomatoes, peeled and chopped (or 1 can crushed San Marzano)

- 1 tablespoon tomato paste

- ½ cup extra virgin olive oil

- ½ cup dry white wine

- 2 tablespoons chopped fresh parsley

- 1 teaspoon dried oregano

- Salt and freshly ground pepper to taste

- Lemon wedges, for serving

HOW TO MAKE IT

1. Preheat the oven to 375°F (190°C).

   Place a heavy enameled cast-iron cocotte (French oven or other heatproof, covered pan over medium heat. Add the olive oil and onions. Cook slowly, stirring often, until the onions are soft and just beginning to caramelize, about 20 minutes.

2. Make the sauce. Add garlic; cook 1 minute. Stir in tomatoes and tomato paste, then pour in the wine. Season lightly with salt, pepper, and oregano. Simmer uncovered 15 minutes until the mixture thickens slightly and the wine loses its sharpness.

3. Assemble. Taste the sauce; adjust seasoning. Push the sauce to the sides and lay the fish fillets in a single layer in the center. Spoon some sauce over each piece until just covered.

4. Bake. Cover with the lid and transfer to the oven. Bake 20–25 minutes. Remove the lid and continue 10 minutes more, allowing the surface to caramelize lightly.

5. Rest and finish. Remove from the oven and let stand 10 minutes. Drizzle with a little fresh olive oil and scatter with parsley. Serve warm with lemon wedges and crusty bread to soak up the sauce.

Servings: 4
Prep Time: 15 minutes
Cook Time: 45
Total Time: 1 hour
Adaptations/Notes: Page 177

CHAPTER ELEVEN
The Taverna

AUGUST 17, 1945. SAN FRANCISCO BAY

With Nickolas still aboard, the thousands of soldiers aboard the USS Admiral C. F. Hughes finally got their first glimpse of the Embarcadero waterfront.

The war had formally ended, and the ship was carrying as many returning servicemen from the Pacific as it could fit onboard. There was not a single empty barrack. The halls, heads, food line, everything was more crowded than ever. V-J Day had been just two days before. It was the first peacetime arrival.

Nickolas missed the birth of his daughter by only hours.

August 17, 1945: Nickolas missed the birth of his daughter by just hours. "I'd have beat the stork if we came in on time," he joked.

That daughter was me.

My father had finally returned to us, to civilian life.

Mom said he looked older than the man in the framed photograph on their dresser. That had been her only glimpse of him for so long.

He stood in the doorway for the longest time, as if uncertain whether he still belonged there. Or maybe he wanted to cross that threshold as a version of himself he couldn't yet find.

Tommy ran to him and clung to his leg.

"Hiya, son. You're a sight for sore eyes, little buddy." His voice was almost a whisper.

No answer, he just clung to Dad's leg as hard as his little arms could.

Dad patted his back absently, eyes still fixed on the room ahead.

Then he noticed me asleep in my little floor seat. He set his bag down and walked toward me, eyes full of wonder.

"Does she know who I am, Mary?"

I was two days old.

"She knows," my mother said, calm and certain. He laughed, though his voice caught, and replied, "Well, I don't."

At least some version of him was home for the holidays that year. Mom said he was unusually quiet at first. For him, that was uncharacteristic.

Dr. Nick Chester, in his military uniform, with my mother, Mary, in an undated photo, circa 1945.

Dad was always polite, but even please and thank you sounded different for a while. Loud and deliberate, as if responding "yes sir" to a commanding officer. She said it felt so strange to see so many men around. To her, it seemed like the whole town was learning what peace felt like again.

ROAST LAMB WITH MANESTRA
MARY CHESTER'S RECIPE

INGREDIENTS

- 1 leg of lamb (about 5–6 pounds)

- 6 cloves garlic, sliced

- Salt and freshly ground black pepper, to taste

- 1 package (16 ounces) orzo pasta

- 1 can (15 ounces) tomato sauce

- 1–2 cups lamb pan juices (from roasting)

- Water, as needed

- Grated Kefalotyri cheese, for serving*

HOW TO MAKE IT

1. Preheat oven to 350°F (175°C).

2. Prepare the lamb: Cut small slits all over the leg and insert slices of garlic. Season generously with salt and pepper. Place in a roasting pan. Do not use glass.

3. Roast until the internal temperature reaches 130°F (54°C) for medium-rare, about 1½ to 2 hours depending on size. Transfer to a platter and rest for 15–20 minutes. Reserve pan juices.

4. Make the manestra: Skim everything left in the roasting pan. Add tomato sauce, several cups of water, salt, and pepper to taste. Stir in orzo and bring to a gentle boil on the stovetop. Reduce heat to low and simmer, stirring frequently, until the orzo is tender and has absorbed most of the liquid, about 15–20 minutes. Add water as needed to prevent sticking.

5. Adjust consistency: The mixture can be served slightly loose, as some prefer, or thicker if allowed to absorb more liquid off the heat.

6. Serve: Spoon manestra onto plates and top with slices of lamb. Sprinkle with grated Kefalotyri cheese.

* Kefalotyri cheese is more traditionally Greek, but Mary was known to use grated Parmigiano-Reggiano. We won't tell.

-

Servings: 6–8
Prep Time: 15 minutes
Cook Time: 2 hours
Total Time: 2 hours 15 minutes
Adaptations/Notes: Page 178

GOOD FRIDAY. 1948. THE CHESTER RESIDENCE

The plates were cleared. My brother and I ran off with our visiting cousins, Belle following to keep an eye on us.

It was just my mom, dad, and his parents at the table then.

"Mary," Kyrios Thomas said softly, "don't wash the dishes now. Please sit for a minute."

My mother put down the plate she had been holding and sunk back into her chair. She was already worried; this didn't sound good.

Kyrios Thomas continued. "Soon, I'll be joining my beautiful wife Maria in heaven."

A chorus of quiet nos. Everyone at the table shook their head as if wishing it to be untrue would change my grandfather's message.

"No, no, please do not feel sorry for me," he went on. "All of my dreams have come true. Look." He gestured toward our big backyard, where we, his grandchildren, were playing.

"I came to this country. I was a business owner," he pronounced the word slowly, with modest pride, "I put my son through dental school. With God's grace, and my dear son's help, I opened another store."

He turned to his son. "Nickolas, by God's grace, you were unharmed in the terrible war, and came home to start a family. You gave me a daughter-in-law who is as beautiful inside as she is on the outside. I have equally beautiful grandchildren. You bought a beautiful mountain cabin right by the lake in Big Bear.

Throughout it all, I had my lovely wife by my side until God called her home two years ago." He crossed himself. "I'm a lucky man. I've truly lived." I can feel my body wishing for permanent sleep, yet I am at peace. There is nothing more I need from this earth. I am already completely blessed. It is time for me to go home."

There was silence at the table. Kyrios Thomas was not a man given to many words; hearing so many at once felt momentous.

There was more. He looked at Nickolas.

"Son, there is one thing your mother and I always wanted to tell you. Now that she is gone, I am the only one left who can give a lovely woman credit where it is due."

He wasn't quite making sense.

"Father Petros told Mrs. Kanakis the Tsetsos boy might leave school. I don't know how he found out.

She never said anything to Belle, but she couldn't bear the thought of your future and Mary's future being destroyed by mere dollars. It was she who gave me the final tuition so that you could finish at university."

A fork slipped out of Mary's hand as a tear formed in her eye. Dear Mrs. Kanakis, her childhood neighbor in Lake Elsinore. She had been gone for years, but was still fondly remembered. That woman had secured their entire future with one kind gesture.

Kyrios Thomas Tsetsos, circa 1946.

"Papa Thomas," she said softly, emotionally, "if you see her when you get to heaven, please thank her for me."

After the war, Los Angeles changed. Contractors built entire neighborhoods of small bungalow homes. National chains like Safeway and Vons began to open large stores with parking lots, fluorescent lights, and weekly ads. They carried anything a shopper would need. Including chocolates and candies. Specialty chains like See's Candies and Fuller's Nut Products started to spring up everywhere. Even the department stores started stocking their shelves with Whitman's Samplers.

Louis felt the squeeze. He tried to look the other way as long as he could. Finally, he couldn't ignore the reality; independent confectioners like him were being pushed aside. He couldn't compete with the modern, sparkling interiors. He didn't have the purchasing power to buy bulk ingredients at enough of a discount to price his goods competitively.

Louis Harrison and his wife Penelope at the tavern they owned, in an undated photo taken sometime in the late 1940s

So, after generations of candy making, he set aside the trays of sugared almonds and chocolates. He closed the candy store, and in its place, he opened a tavern. It was a different kind of trade, but it suited him. Men came in after long shifts to share a drink, tell stories, argue, and laugh. The bar hummed with life in a way the candy shop never had. Louis had left behind the world of confections, but not the spirit of hospitality. He poured, he listened, he joked.

He would walk home in the evenings thinking that the shift hadn't been as difficult as he anticipated. It was a shame that he had to break generations of traditions, though. He thought of his father and grandfather, back in Greece. He hadn't written his old man in a while. He decided he would write a letter the next day.

METAXA SIDECAR
LOUIS' VERSION OF THIS SMOOTH, CLASSIC COCKTAIL

INGREDIENTS

- 2 oz Metaxa (5-Star or 7-Star)

- ¾ oz orange liqueur, many use Gran Marinier but Louis preferred Cointreau over all others

- ¾ oz freshly squeezed lemon juice

- Ice cubes

- Sugar for the rim (optional)

- Lemon twist or orange peel, to garnish (Louis preferred to serve his with a lemon twist)

HOW TO MAKE IT

1. Prepare the glass: If desired, lightly moisten the rim of a chilled coupe or cocktail glass with lemon juice and dip in sugar.

2. Mix the drink: In a cocktail shaker, combine Metaxa, Cointreau, and lemon juice. Fill with ice.

3. Shake well: Shake vigorously until well-chilled, about 15 seconds.

4. Strain and serve: Strain into the prepared glass. Garnish with a twist of lemon or orange peel.

This is Louis' take on the traditional Sidecar cocktail, using Metaxa (a Greek amber spirit made from brandy blended with aged wine and botanicals) instead of cognac.

In the summer, this is refreshing and ideal as-is. In the fall and winter, add a small pinch of pumpkin pie spice or ¼ oz pumpkin spice syrup pumpkin spice syrup for warmth. Avoid overpowering to keep it balanced.

Servings: 1
Prep Time: 5 minutes
Total Time: 5 minutes
Adaptations/Notes: Page 178

Anyway, he reasoned, as long as the tavern business paid the bills, it didn't really matter. Home life was fine. Their children were growing. Their youngest, Dean was fourteen now. Lanky and restless, beginning to unconsciously display hints of the man he would become. He already stood taller than his father and older brothers.

MEZEDES
SMALL PLATE MEZE SPREAD FOR GUESTS

INGREDIENTS

- Loukaniko (Greek sausage): Fried or grilled slices, rich with pork fat, orange peel, and fennel.

- Kefalotyri cheese: Hard, salty, sheep's milk cheese, cut thick.

- Pan-fried sykotaki (Greek liver delicacy): Common meze plate, sautéed in olive oil with onions.

- Salted sardines or anchovies: Oily, briny fish to balance the beer.

- Eggs kokkinista: Hard-boiled eggs simmered briefly in tomato and oil, served warm.

- Olives & pickled peppers: Sharp, salty counterpoints.

- Thick, artisan bread: Slices to mop up the oils, cheeses, and sauces.

HOW TO MAKE IT

LOUKÁNIKO (GREEK SAUSAGE)

1. Heat olive oil in a skillet over medium heat.

2. Fry sausage slices until browned and aromatic, about 5–7 minutes.

PAN-FRIED SYKOTAKI (GREEK LIVER DELICACY)

1. In a separate skillet, heat olive oil.

2. Add onions and sauté until soft, about 5 minutes.

3. Add liver pieces and cook until browned outside and just tender inside, 5–6 minutes more.

4. Season with salt and pepper.

EGGS KOKKINISTÁ

1. Heat olive oil in a small pan, add tomato sauce, and season with salt, pepper, and cinnamon.

2. Add halved hard-boiled eggs and simmer gently for 5 minutes.

ARRANGE THE PLATTER

1. Arrange the items artfully a large board or serving tray, Decorate with rosemary or basil sprigs, or freshly-washed edible flowers.

2. Serve warm.

Subsitute freely as ingredients are in season and freshly available.

Serves: 6–8 as an appetizer spread
Prep Time: 20 minutes
Cook Time: 25 minutes
Total Time: 45 minutes
Adaptations/Notes: Page 179

FEBRUARY 1953. THE HARRISON RESIDENCE

Penelope admired her husband's resilience. He was quickly adapting to the differences between a candy shop and a tavern. Weekends were getting busier, and Louis was devising ways to entice more customers to stop by on the weeknights, which were slower.

He spoke of new libations she had never heard of. Whiskey sours, highballs, boilermakers, Cuba libres, gin and tonic, and, of course, Nickolas' favorite, Seven and Seven. Penelope marveled at all of the colorful labels. There were more than one hundred bottles behind the bar.

For his favorite customers, Louis would offer an off-menu special. His own rendition of the Metaxa sidecar.

One Wednesday, Louis came home later than usual. Penelope watched from a chair where she had been doing a bit of needlepoint as he came through the door. He was a little unsteady on his feet, but his face was flushed with cheer. He told her with a grin that the happy hour special he offered had been a big success. The tavern had been packed, which was unheard of mid-week.

Later that evening, two of his Greek buddies had stopped by just before closing. They were truly glad for Louis, and the three of them celebrated by enjoying several Metaxa sidecars themselves. Louis brought out small plate after small plate of meze. They nibbled and drank, before heading home.

Penelope hugged him tightly, feeling relieved, then helped him get to bed. Within minutes, he was snoring. She watched him sleep. She had always loved to do that.

There wasn't a man in Los Angeles that deserved a break more than Louis, she believed.

She didn't wake him the next day. She had prepared his usual breakfast, toasted Greek sesame bread topped with kefalotyri cheese and drizzled lightly with honey. Louis loved the balance of the salty cheese and the sweetness of the honey. It was a perfect complement to the strong, Greek coffee he preferred.

Their son Nick's wife had asked if she could watch her granddaughter that morning.

Young Penny asked to skip the cheese and just have bread with honey. Her yia-yia happily obliged. She sat on the opposite side of the kitchen table, bouncing in her chair and humming while she nibbled on her food.

Louis' breakfast sat on the table, untouched, for quite a while. He finally appeared, mid-morning and sat down. She looked over at him. He looked pale. Penelope knew he had been drinking the night before, but he hadn't been nearly drunk enough to have a hangover. Then it happened. A sudden clutching at his chest, the sound of the chair scraping hard against the floor as he lurched to the side, and fell to the ground. The newspaper slid to the floor beside him. Penny shrieked in horror. His breath caught once, twice, then failed.

The dishcloth Penelope had been holding fell to the ground as she watched, horrified. For a heartbeat she did not move.

She thought he had lost his balance, that he might steady himself again. Maybe he was dizzy. But the color drained from his face. She rushed to him, calling his name, her voice rising in panic, her hands reaching for his arm, his shoulder. He did not answer. His weight fell against her, heavy and unresponsive. Penny was sobbing loudly. Dean and Mary Anne heard the commotion and came running, their voices crowding the air with questions, fear.

Penelope's world narrowed to the sight before her: Louis, the man who had steadied her in every moment, slipping away where she could not follow.

Then there was only stillness.

The ticking clock. The leaves outside.

Louis was gone.

It had been a massive heart attack. Sudden, final. By the time the ambulance arrived, it was too late. The man who had once blushed when asked the time, who had turned sugar into sweetness and strangers into friends, was gone in an instant.

Penelope sat on the kitchen floor, her hand still on his sleeve, waiting for something to come back to her. Breath. Warmth. A pulse. It did not.

The shock hollowed them all. Penelope, widowed at forty-eight, stood at the center of a home that had lost its gravity. Dean, still half boy and half man, stared at the doorway as if his father might yet walk through it. The daughters clung to one another and whispered prayers.

Neighbors came with casseroles, but grief has no appetite.

CHAPTER TWELVE

Ascension

1954. INGLEWOOD, CALIFORNIA

Penelope's son Nick did his best to help. But they were in financial dire straits. The tavern had to be closed and they had bills to pay.

At home now, it was just Marcy, Venita and Dean, who was fourteen at the time.

They all went to work. The daughters, in offices. Dean lied about his age, and managed to get a job collecting carts at the local supermarket. His sisters and mother grieved, but he felt angry and alone. It was a rainy winter that year. He would shiver he pushed lines of cold, heavy shopping carts back inside the store.

They were tough years. Lean, and long. Dean would never really get over the loss of his father, whom he adored, at such a young age. Penelope felt the worst for him when he played football in high school and his father was not on the sidelines to watch. Sitting on the chilly bleachers, she could hear echoes of Louis' enthusiastic cheers as she watched her son on the field. She knew nothing about the sport.

That house became a place of survival and ritual. Nick had three children of his own, but he'd stop by on his way home from work to check in on his mother. As the oldest son, he was the "man of the house" now. The daughters had busy office jobs downtown. Penelope and Dean could get by with the simplest of meals.

Later, Dean said that he had made a vow to himself, right there in that supermarket parking lot, not to be "poor" anymore. Hard work ran in the family, and eventually he would make good on the promise he made to himself. Like his brothers, he had ambition. He graduated high school and was accepted to the UCLA school of engineering.

He worked all the while, selling men's suits, then later, large movie cameras to television studios.

My parents gave my brother and me everything they didn't have themselves. I was a debutante. Tommy got a new car and a guitar. I was Greek Queen, a kind of homecoming event the Greek-American Youth Association used to hold. They paid for both of us to attend college. More importantly, they were involved in all the right ways.

Before we could drive, my father took my friends and me anywhere we needed to be. I don't remember why, but we all called him "Noodle." I thought he was the best dad on the block. My mother supported every activity we wanted to try. She understood the culture, and she was only strict when she needed to be. School dances, football games, and nights at the local soda fountain were smiled upon. She wanted us to enjoy our teen years. The more wholesome fun we had, the better.

Dean was six years older. He had lost his father young, and his mother had seven other children before him. He grew up with everything he needed but there was no room for extras. His sister Marcy, with money from her office job, once took him on a bus to get to an orthodontist. She paid out of her own pocket for him get braces on his teeth. Without her help, he might have gone without.

We were two people who attended the same high school, although not at the same time. We grew up just a mile or so away from one another. Yet, in retrospect, I realize I wasn't just unacquainted with Dean personally. I didn't even know him in an empirical sense.

We met through mutual church friends. The 1960s were in full swing. Beatles the band and Beetles the cars. He was street-wise, I was innocent. I enrolled at the California State University, Long Beach (CSULB) and moved into the dorms there. I wore my hair with a middle part, straight and long.

The iconic 1960s go-go boots were a wardrobe staple. My miniskirts were as short as my parents would allow, which wasn't nearly as short as a lot of the girls wore them. Burn my bra in protest? With traditional Greek parents? Forget it. He told me he thought I looked like the actress Ali MacGraw.

My father, Nickolas, had high hopes that I would marry a Greek man. He wanted to hold on to our culture if he could. Dean was bold. He carried himself with the loose-shouldered swagger of someone who didn't care if the world approved. He had that dangerous kind of charm, the sort you knew better than to trust, but found hard to ignore. There was a flicker of rebellion in everything he did. It worked for him. It worked for my dad. He loved Dean.

After my father's parents, Kyrios Thomas and Kyria Maria, passed away, my maternal grandma, Belle, moved in with us. For a time, I had to share a room with her. As a teen, I thought sharing a bed with her was pretty awful. My parents shrugged. It was the "Greek way," they were used to it.

If you recall, my mother Mary was already an accomplished cook when she married him. Her mother, Belle, was equally talented in the kitchen. Together, they were nearly identical to Penelope's own mother and grandmother back in the old country, in Koroni.

As a girl, in our kitchen, I watched them create meals effortlessly side by side. Skill was taken for granted. Even culinary school graduates rarely leave with such a sense of balance: their dishes were rich yet never heavy, their textures crisp where they should be and tender where they need to be. Perfectly roasted, sauteed, simmered, or grilled. Recipes were for amateurs.

DOLMADES
STUFFED GRAPE LEAVES

INGREDIENTS

MAIN DISH

- 1 ½ pounds ground beef
- 1 onion, finely chopped
- 3 cloves garlic, minced
- ½ cup uncooked white rice
- 1 tablespoon olive oil
- 2 large eggs
- 1 jar (about 60) grape leaves, rinsed and drained
- Salt and pepper, to taste
- Avgolemono sauce (for serving)

AVGOLEMONO SAUCE

- 2 large eggs
- Juice of 2 lemons

HOW TO MAKE IT

MAIN DISH

1. In a large bowl, combine the beef, onion, garlic, rice, olive oil, eggs, salt, and pepper. Mix gently until evenly combined.

2. Lay a grape leaf shiny side down on a flat surface. Trim and discard the hard stem. Place about 1 teaspoon of filling near the stem end of the leaf.

3. Fold the sides of the leaf over the filling, then roll up tightly from the bottom to form a neat cylinder. Repeat with remaining leaves and filling.

4. Line the bottom of a large pot with a few unused grape leaves to prevent sticking. Arrange the stuffed leaves seam side down in tight layers.

5. Add enough water to just cover the dolmades. Place a heatproof plate on top to keep them submerged.

6. Bring to a gentle simmer over medium-low heat. Cover and cook for about 1 hour, until the rice and meat are tender.

7. Serve warm or at room temperature with avgolemono sauce spooned generously over the top.

AVGOLEMONO SAUCE

8. In a bowl, whisk eggs and lemon juice until frothy.

9. Gradually add a ladleful of hot broth from the pot while whisking constantly to temper the eggs.

10. Slowly pour the egg–lemon mixture back into the pot, stirring gently.

Omit ground beef entirely for vegetarian option. For other diets, ground pork, turkey, chicken or finely chopped cod, sea bass or shrimp are also commonly used, depending on the region.

Servings: About 30–40 dolmades
Prep Time: 40 minutes
Cook Time: 1 hour
Total Time: 1 hour 40 minutes
Adaptations/Notes: Page 180

I know it sounds cliché, but history sure does have a way of repeating itself. Two cooks in Penelope's childhood kitchen. She never learned to cook. Two cooks in my childhood kitchen.

True story: I called my mom, Mary, from my first apartment and asked her how to boil an egg.

My family, the Chesters, did know the Harrisons through church and such. When my relationship with Dean started to be something more than just a few dates, he'd bring me to Penelope's house now and then for dinner. Penelope would be in the kitchen, wearing a housedress with an apron over it.

I recall being at the table. Marcy was there, along with Penelope, Dean and me. The subject of cooking came up. Not in terms of "if," but rather "what" I like to cook. Dean had never asked me about cooking. With our wedding just months away, it was time to come clean.

Times had changed so much since Penelope had felt shame about her lack of cooking skills. I was a student at university, and would later have a career of my own. Still, in that moment, none of it mattered. I felt nervous. I had to tell them I didn't know how to cook. At all.

I blurted it out. I'm sure it came out very awkwardly.

But Penelope just smiled, with a faraway look in her eyes. She had been there once herself, standing in her own kitchen as a young bride, clumsy with pots and pans, not knowing how to season a roast or knead bread. Where another woman might have offered all of the criticism, the judgment, that I expected, Penelope offered kindness. She had no scorn to give. Only memories.

"Come early next time," she said. "You come by yourself. Dean can come later."

CHAPTER THIRTEEN

A House of Pastry

1966. LOS ANGELES

Penelope taught me with expert hands, and also sweet humor.

Meanwhile, Dean and I moved in to our first apartment in Redondo Beach, then bought a house. He had dropped out of college at UCLA, but we were doing really well financially. He was finally in a position to be able to help his mother, Penelope. At that point, just two sisters were left at home, Marcy and Venita.

Dean and his siblings helped the three of them buy a house in the Del Rey neighborhood of Los Angeles.

Their new house had a really nice kitchen.

Penelope, like all proper grieving Greek widows at the time, wore black to church for the remainder of her life. Yet, everyone agreed that it was that very kitchen that gave her a new lease on life.

Cooking became a different kind of necessity. It became a way of holding everyone together. Counters and tables everywhere disappeared under parchment, rows of pastries waiting to be baked. The place was alive, every corner carrying the scent of butter, spices, and honey.

And visit after visit, she tied an apron around my waist, the same gesture her mother and grandmother had once made to her in a faraway village. Science tells us that memory deepens when anchored in the body, when hands repeat what eyes observe. That was how Penelope had learned, not from paper, but from repetition. Now I, too, began to learn by heart.

Over time, something larger than recipes passed between us. She knew things I didn't. She was teaching me empowerment, confidence, more than how to braise lamb or roll out phyllo dough. I learned from her how to trust my senses, how to make order from raw ingredients, how to find resilience in the rhythm of kneading, tasting, correcting, beginning again.

We laughed at mistakes, got to know and love one another over simmering pots, and in time, this bride who once felt intimidated standing before a stove became a woman who could command a kitchen on her own.

Dean and I got married.

All of the Harrisons and all of the Chesters were there. We honeymooned in Hawaii, bought a few homes, and had daughters. Dean continued to succeed in his professional life.

The years with Penelope as my mother-in-law were rich in ways I came to fully understand later. She was steady, humble, and full of quiet wisdom. She would smile and laugh at small missteps.

We shared countless meals, small celebrations, and long afternoons in her kitchen. Side by side, we understood one another without words.

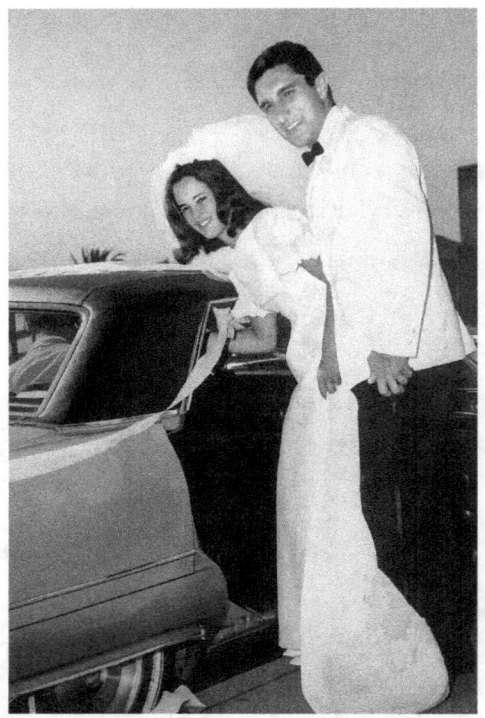

The author and Penelope's youngest son, Dean, on their wedding day in 1966.

I began writing down what she couldn't. Initially, I did it so that I could replicate the dishes at home, for my own family. Later, I realized I had preserved an entire heritage without even realizing it. One I would not have known as well if we had never connected.

But we both soon saw that success was changing my husband, her son. He grew unpredictable, his moods sharper, his temper shorter.

1974. ROLLING HILLS ESTATES

Dean never lost touch with two of his closest friends from UCLA. Together, the three of them were extraordinarily handsome, confident men with money in their pockets and a way of drawing attention wherever they went. They were each other's wingmen in nightclub after nightclub, married men, behaving like bachelors.

He worked long hours all week, rarely seeing our children. The girls were always asleep by the time he came home, and when they weren't, he was very impatient and short with them. When the weekend came, there were always the boys' nights out: Friday and Saturday both. Sunday was spent at church, followed by brunch with the family. By the time we returned home, the weekend was over, and so were our chances at time together. I got the sense he didn't mind.

His brothers, Nick and Harry, knew too. They'd seen him around town with his arms around beautiful women.

Eight years later, we stood face to face in the entryway of our house in the hills. It was very late. He had just come home and, as usual after those nights out, he'd had more than a few drinks. Through the expansive windows, the city lights sprawled beneath us, Los Angeles glittering with all the places he might have been that night. A friend had called earlier. She and her husband had eaten dinner at a popular new restaurant. She apologized through tears as she confirmed what I already knew: he had been unfaithful. It wasn't the first time.

He hadn't expected me to still be awake. I told him I wanted a divorce, then turned quietly and went to bed.

They were words I never thought I'd have to say. I lay there in the dark, listening to my own thoughts. Surprisingly, they weren't about Dean, or the marriage. Not about fear of what came next, or of being alone.

I thought only of how to tell my girls. My mother and father. The rest of the family. My happily married friends.

Each disappointed face appeared in my mind as if I were already in the room with them.

I had managed to finish college while married and pregnant with my oldest daughter. I had a degree now, and a career ahead of me. I'd be fine, in a sense.

Yet, I'll never forget saying goodbye to Penelope. It was harder than saying goodbye to Dean.

Penelope Harrison, 1972.

She already knew. There were no need for words. We embraced for the longest time, and shared genuine tears of a loss we knew was coming. Looking back now, it's hard to fathom how different things were then. It was another era. It no longer felt right to continue visiting and cooking side by side as if nothing had changed. Our time had been cut short by a fate we knew was a reality but hadn't had the heart to accept.

She lived for another thirty-eight years after her dear Louis' passing. I am so glad she was able to find her light again. So grateful for the years we spent together.

CHAPTER FOURTEEN

Their Just Desserts

My father, Nickolas continued to sing in barbershop quartets and act in local plays. Throughout the years, he stayed in contact with the friends he made in the military's selective service during World War II.

Greek-Americans chose him by the hundreds as their dentist, even if they had to drive a long way for an appointment. They felt comfortable communicating with him, and he made thousands of friends that way.

He also remained active at his alma mater, USC. In 1969, he briefly served as president of the dental school's alumni association. He had seen his old classmates several times over the years at reunions and such, but this one gathering stuck out in his mind.

He had just finished addressing the group and stepped down from the podium to applause and a few whistles. Wallace and Rice were walking his way, grinning.

"Nicky! Look at you, Mr. President!" Wallace said, shaking his hand hard.

He laughed. "They'll figure out their mistake soon enough."

Rice chuckled. "Nah, you always were the golden boy."

Nickolas shook his head. "Hardly."

They talked for a while. Professors long gone, who had retired where. Remember so-and-so? Then Rice leaned in. "Hey, you ever hear about Woodard?"

Nickolas stared at his old friend. Rice looked serious, which was rare. "No. What about him?"

Wallace's smile faded. He had been the closest of the three to Woodard, and never one to exaggerate. "Lost his license. Painkillers. Writing scripts under fake names. Whole thing blew up on him. Papers said he was hooked himself by the end."

"Jheezzzus," Nickolas said quietly, shaking his head.

Rice nodded. "Yeah. Shame. Smart guy, too."

Nickolas didn't say anything at first. "He really was," he finally said. "Always trying too hard."

Wallace shrugged. "Guess we all were, back then."

Nickolas gave a small nod. "Yeah. Some of us just never stopped."

They stood there a moment, until someone called Wallace over for a photo. They said their goodbyes, and Nickolas headed toward the coffee urn, thinking about how strange it was. First, how odd it was to be called "golden boy." He guessed they couldn't tell how different it was to be an immigrant.

He had tried hard because he had to. He never forgot what it was like to be barely hanging on. He needed the education, but his parents did too, in a sense. Every decision they had made since he was five years old had banked upon his success.

He stepped outside to cool off, and lit a cigarette. His thoughts shifted to Woodard, and the way time sorted men out all on its own.

He felt relieved that he had landed on the right side of whatever it was that those early years had tried to take from him. There was no way of knowing at the time, but he had the right parents, picked the right school, the right wife. Still, the years tried to take and take. A lot of it was just pure luck.

His father had left him the stores in his will, which had been taken over by a new proprietor twenty or so years before. He used to make the trip once a month to check on the places and collect the rent in person. He liked the tenant. But after the Watts riots, he wasn't able to go there anymore. The neighborhood was just too dangerous for him.

As you might recall, he had always traded chocolate for cigarettes while he was in the service. He finally did manage to stop smoking toward the end of his life, but we lost him too soon.

1980s. REDONDO BEACH, CALIFORNIA

My mother Mary, like Penelope with Louis, grieved the loss of her husband of forty-three years. She lived twenty-seven years after Nickolas' passing.

It took time, but she eventually found new footing.

For a while, she'd host the Greek traditional Anastasi meal. To many, this is the most festive occasion of the year. Most Greeks consider the Easter holiday the most celebratory of all.

They end the Lenten period of fasting and reflection by attending midnight services at the cathedral. For a lot of people this is the only time of the year they go to church, so the vast sanctuary fills to maximum capacity. Typically, the church is so crowded that even standing room is unavailable and the last to arrive are forced to watch the service on monitors in the narthex or other rooms, livestreamed from the altar. Beyond Easter's religious importance, the service is cherished for its meaning and beauty.

It's such a major event that local police are parked outside. Sometimes, they use traffic cones to direct all of the cars before and after the service.

When the parishioners arrive, they quietly take their seats in a darkened nave. To get an actual seat, they would have had to come early, so they wait. Around 11:30 pm, a hush comes over the crowd, the priest emerges, chanting low and somber. All but the scarcest lighting remains off, so they listen in the dark. It is hauntingly somber, recalling the darkness of the tomb before dawn breaks, the stillness before Resurrection.

Quietly, helpers make their way down the center and side aisles, baskets in hand. They pass out candles. Everyone gets one.

Midnight arrives. Bells ring. The priest begins by lighting a single candle in celebration of the Resurrection. He uses that tiny flame to light the candle of another. Gradually, worshipers pass the flame from one to another. What follows feels almost otherworldly. One flame becomes hundreds. Slowly, the cathedral begins to glow, flickering with golden candlelight. Eventually, the darkness is gone and the priest begins chanting and announcing with jubilation that "Christ has truly risen."

The air shifts from lamentation to jubilation. The words "Christos Anésti" echo through the nave.

ARNI FRICASSEE
MARY'S BRAISED LAMB WITH AVGOLEMONO SAUCE

INGREDIENTS

MAIN DISH

- 3 pounds lamb shoulder or leg, cut into large chunks

- 2 tablespoons olive oil

- 1 large onion, finely chopped

- 2 bunches green onions, chopped

- 2 heads romaine lettuce, coarsely chopped

- 2–3 sprigs fresh dill, chopped

- 1 teaspoon salt

- ½ teaspoon freshly ground black pepper

- 5 cups water or light chicken stock

AVGOLEMONO SAUCE

- 2 large eggs

- Juice of 2 lemons

HOW TO MAKE IT

MAIN DISH

1. Brown the lamb: In a large pot, heat olive oil over medium heat. Add lamb and brown on all sides until golden. Remove and set aside.

2. Sauté aromatics: In the same pot, add onion and green onions. Sauté until softened, about 5 minutes. Return the lamb to the pot.

3. Add greens: Stir in romaine lettuce and dill. Cook until the lettuce wilts slightly.

4. Simmer: Add water or chicken stock, salt, and pepper. Bring to a boil, then reduce heat to low. Cover and simmer until the lamb is tender, about 1 hour.

AVGOLEMONO SAUCE

5. In a bowl, whisk eggs and lemon juice until frothy.

6. Gradually add a ladleful of hot broth from the pot while whisking constantly to temper the eggs.

7. Slowly pour the egg–lemon mixture back into the pot, stirring gently.

ASSEMBLE AND SERVE

8. Warm gently over low heat (do not boil) until the sauce thickens slightly and coats the lamb.

9. Adjust seasoning and serve immediately.

Avgolemono sauce is this dish's superpower. It is vegetarian and dairy-free, yet reads as a creamy, tangy sauce. It is used throughout Greek cooking. If you're vegetarian, or prefer other proteins to lamb, you can make it on its own and use it so many ways.

Servings: 6
Prep Time: 25 minutes
Cook Time: 1 hour 20 minutes
Total Time: 1 hour 45 minutes
Adaptations/Notes: Page 180

The emotionally resonant, purely joyous air is infectious. People stream out of the church, candles still lit. Traditionally, you're supposed to try to keep it lighted all the way home. So we would be careful not to let the flames go out, laughing softly at the sight of ourselves holding burning candles in the car as we drove home in the pre-dawn darkness.

Mary would be with us of course, but she would have spent hours in advance, preparing the meal. We would have been fasting in the days leading up to this holy night, and would arrive hungry. Remember, the service doesn't culminate until midnight. It's nearly dawn now, yet the biggest celebration of the year is just beginning. All the lights are on, wine is being poured, and everyone is celebrating.

Traditionally, at this resurrection meal, a specific type of soup called magiritsa would be served. I know putting these words into print will alleviate some guilt of many expatriate Greeks: Mary was never a fan herself, nor would her blended family of Americans have ever been happy to be served a porridge of lamb offal (liver, heart, lungs, and intestines). Still, Mary realized that reverence defined the day, above all things. Avgolemono, found in both soup and sauce form in this book, is a traditional part of the meal. She would borrow the concept of lamb from the magiritsa, and pair it with avgolemono sauce.

DIPLES HONEY-FRIED PASTRIES

TRADITIONAL PELOPONNESIAN CELEBRATION SWEET

INGREDIENTS

DOUGH

- 4 large eggs

- 1 tablespoon sugar

- 1 tablespoon brandy or ouzo

- 1 teaspoon baking soda

- 1 teaspoon vinegar (to activate the soda)

- ¼ teaspoon salt

- 2 cups all-purpose flour, plus extra for dusting

- Olive oil, for frying

SYRUP COATING

- 1 cup honey

- ½ cup water

- ½ cup sugar

- 1 small cinnamon stick

- Strip of lemon peel

GARNISH

- ½ cup finely chopped walnuts

- 1 teaspoon ground cinnamon

HOW TO MAKE IT

MAIN DISH

1. Make the dough: In a large bowl, beat eggs and sugar together until pale and thick. Stir in the brandy, baking soda dissolved in vinegar, and salt. Gradually add flour, mixing until a soft, elastic dough forms. Knead briefly on a floured surface, then cover with a cloth and rest 30 minutes.

2. Roll and cut: Divide dough into smaller portions. Using a pasta roller or long dowel, roll each piece into paper-thin sheets, thinner than phyllo if possible. Cut into rectangles about 4×6 inches.

3. Fry and shape: Heat about 1 inch of olive oil in a wide pan over medium-high heat. Working one at a time, drop a rectangle into the hot oil. As soon as it begins to puff, use two forks to roll it into a loose cylinder or spiral while still frying. Remove when golden, drain briefly on paper towels, and repeat.

4. Prepare the syrup: In a small saucepan, combine honey, water, sugar, cinnamon stick, and lemon peel. Bring to a gentle boil and simmer 5 minutes. Remove the cinnamon stick and peel.

5. Finish and serve: Dip each dipla into the warm syrup for a few seconds, coating all sides. Arrange on a platter. Sprinkle generously with chopped walnuts and cinnamon. Serve the same day for crispness.

Servings: About 25
Prep Time: 1 hour
Cook Time: 30 minutes
Total Time: 1 hour 30 minutes
Adaptations/Notes: Page 181

Mary was now alone in their sprawling ranch house. It was high up in the hills, sitting atop a vast deep canyon lush with greenery and interwoven with horse trails where people would frequently ride. Ironically, just on the other side of that canyon was the home where Dean and I once lived, that fateful night that I told him I wanted to end our marriage. To me, the memory of that canyon will always represent some sort of existential divide.

She was very close with her neighbors, and just a mile or two from the country club where she liked to play golf. Still, it was isolated and quiet there. So, several years after my dad's passing, she made the difficult decision to put the family home up for sale.

It turned out to be one of the best decisions of her later years. Instead of buying a new home, she opted to simply rent a small apartment, right on the beach, where she had large circles of friends. She hardly ever needed her car. Shopping and restaurants were all within walking distance, and my mother loved to walk. She continued to play golf, traveled, and in the evenings she took up line dancing.

Men were interested in her, but she never felt compelled to date. Her explanation made sense.

"I've taken care of people all my life," she told me in her late sixties.

"Men my age want a housewife. I took care of his parents, my parents, and my own family. It's time for me to be free."

Only after dad's passing did she open up about her childhood on the ranch. There had been some dark times. Beneath the innocence my father saw in her the day they met, a trait she never lost, there had always been a thoughtful complexity. It was one I know he sensed, but maybe never fully saw. She was different, more fully her. She didn't cook much after that. She didn't need to be anyone anymore. The gifts she had to offer had already been given. It was her time.

2025. COASTAL OREGON

At the time of this writing, I had just celebrated my 80th birthday. I still make meals from time to time, but my time in a busy kitchen, filled with the aromas of my heritage, is mostly behind me now.

What is left is for me to record the memories. They are so much more than simply ingredients. My mother Mary's legacy. Everything my father instinctively knew about her, when he saw her for the first time that day, turned out to be true. Her energy was endless, and she used every spark of it to electrify those she loved. We were aglow just because she was there.

And then, there are all the memories of Penelope. I believe she found new life in old traditions she had left behind in Greece more than a half-century before. She had fifteen grandchildren. She adopted a relatively modern look in the 1950s, with cat-eye glasses in a pearly gray. She wore them long after they went out of fashion, until she passed away at the age of ninety-three.

Penelope left Greece as just a girl. She endured separation, loss, war, heartbreak and hardship. Like so many immigrants, rather than buckling under the pressure, she grew into a matriarch worthy of the dedication to a manuscript like this one.

And so the cycle closed, only to open again. The aprons passed down were the fabric of survival, of laughter, of tears that salted soups and human sweetness that was folded into dough. What had begun as necessity had become heritage. I pass that on to you so that you may pass it on to others.

With affection,from Koroni and Los Angeles.

ABOUT THE AUTHORS

Kathy Crane

Kathy Crane, circa 1950, at home with her parents. Nickolas and Mary Chester.

Kathy Crane built a distinguished career as an executive while raising her daughters on her own. After her marriage to Dean Harrison ended, she rebuilt her life with focus and independence, remaining close and connected to her parents, "Doc" Nick Chester and Mary. Her work took her around the world and cultivated the leadership skills she later brought to public life, serving as Executive Director of the Chamber of Commerce in the coastal Oregon town where she and her husband, George, settled after retirement. Both the vision for this book and the meticulous arrangement of recipies began with her. Projects born from gratitude, memory, and a desire to honor the generations before her.

Sandia Harrison

Sandia Harrison with her paternal grandmother, Penelope, circa 1967.

Sandia Harrison, daughter of Kathy Crane and Dean Harrison, granddaughter of Penelope and Louis, Mary and Nickolas, grew up surrounded by women whose strength, wisdom, and humor defined resilience. A California native whose life has also taken her to London, Denmark, and Chicago, she built a vibrant career while raising her own family and continuing a tradition of community involvement, volunteer work, interesting hobbies, and world travel. Inspired by her mother's vision, the two collaborated to bring this book to life; a shared act of preservation and love across generations. She researched and wrote this while overlooking beautiful Lake Elsinore, a place that brings her family's story full circle.

RECIPE ADAPTATIONS & DIETARY NOTES

There's a certain kind of hospitality that never goes out of fashion. It's the kind rooted in tradition, the type practiced by all the women in this story.

For Penelope, a typical gathering included her seven children, spouses, grandchildren, great-grandchildren, other relatives and close family friends.

Her philosophy, and her table, reflected that it was about more than food.

There was something quietly elegant about the way she adapted without fuss, as though it had always been part of the plan. True tradition isn't rigid; it's generous. And when a hostess honors that spirit, people remember the feeling long after the meal is over.

What follows is a guide to adaptations, substitutions, and considerations for every recipe in this collection.

May everyone who graces your table feel the care you put into every masterpiece you create.

SIDERITIS HERBAL INFUSION (GREEK MOUNTAIN TEA)

Base profile: Naturally caffeine-free herbal infusion made from dried Sideritis (Greek mountain tea), known for its antioxidant and anti-inflammatory properties.
Vegan or sugar-free adaptation: Omit honey.
Full recipe: page 12

HORIATIKI (TRADITIONAL VILLAGE) SALAD

Base profile: Naturally vegetarian, plant based, gluten free, and low fat, this classic salad celebrates the simplicity of pure ingredients with light, flavorful, mildly tangy dressing.
Vegan adaptation: Omit feta cheese or replace it with a plant-based alternative.
Low sodium adaptation: Use low-salt olives or rinse them thoroughly before adding. Omit feta cheese or use very sparingly and reduce salt in dressing.
Full recipe: page 18

GRILLED OCTOPUS WITH LEMON-OLIVE DRESSING (LADOLEMONO)

Base profile: Smoky, briny, faintly sweet from caramelized exterior. Core aromatics are olive oil, red wine vinegar, oregano, bay leaf, peppercorns. There are many regional adaptations.

Lowfat / heart-healthy – "Santorini Style Light" adaptation: Parboil octopus in white wine, garlic, and bay leaf, omit pre-grilling oil. After grilling, drizzle measured olive oil (1 tbsp per serving) rather than marinating. Replace salt with lemon zest and sumac for brightness.

Non-shellfish adaptation: Grilled swordfish cubes or sea bass fillets can be substituted. If making both, be sure to cook seperately.

Full recipe: page 22

AVGOLEMONO SOUP

Base profile: Lemon-forward, rich and satisfying.

For vegetarian adaptation: Substitute vegetable broth for chicken broth. To deepen the flavor so that it is closer to the original intent, add a splash of olive oil and a small pinch of nutritional yeast or a preserved lemon slice.

For vegan adaptation: Replace chicken broth with vegetable broth, omit eggs, and use blended silken tofu or soaked cashews with lemon juice for body.

Chef's note: This dish is naturally gluten and lactose free.

Full recipe: page 26

STIFADO (BRAISED BEEF HERITAGE STEW)

Base profile: Mediterranean, low carb, universally adaptable.

For lighter or vegetarian adaptation: Substitute mushrooms, lentils, or eggplant for beef. Use vegetable broth in place of stock.

For gluten-free adaptation: Ensure tomato paste, vinegar, and wine are certified gluten free, and serve over potatoes, gluten-free pasta, or rice.

For paleo or dairy-free diets: Serve over potatoes or other root vegetables. Use ghee or plant-based butter if desired. The dish is naturally grain- and dairy-free.

Full recipe: page 35

BAKALIAROS SKORDALIÁ

For gluten-free diets: Use a gluten-free flour blend and ensure the fish is dusted lightly before dipping into the batter.

For vegan preparation: Omit the fish; serve Skordaliá with grilled zucchini or cauliflower steaks.

For regional authenticity: In Macedonia, walnuts are added for depth.

Chef's note: The sparkling water batter creates a delicate, crisp crust without heaviness, a hallmark of good Bakaliaros.

Full recipe: page 40

LADI KAI TOMATA (FIVE MINUTE TOMATO DIPPING OIL)

Base profile: The sweetness of tomato paste blends with the peppery oil, the garlic carrying warmth through exhaustion.

Chef's note: Modest, fragrant, comforting, but most of all, fast. It reflects the early immigrant table: whole ingredients transformed into something greater than their sum.

This dish is naturally vegan, vegetarian, dairy-free, Paleo and Keto-friendly, and sugar-free on it's own. The only consideration would be the bread used for dipping.

Full recipe: page 43

FASOLADA SOUP

Base profile: Mediterranean, plant-based, gluten-free, naturally low in fat.

For enhanced protein: Add white beans and lentils in combination, or stir in a spoonful of tahini before serving.

For paleo adaptation: Substitute chickpeas with diced root vegetables such as parsnips or turnips and omit legumes entirely.

For richer flavor without altering the profile: Finish with a drizzle of olive oil or a squeeze of lemon just before serving.

Full recipe: page 51

CHICKEN KAPAMA

This dish is naturally gluten free when served with rice or potatoes instead of orzo, and naturally lactose free as written (omit cheese topping).

For a vegetarian or vegan adaptation, substitute chicken with hearty mushrooms or eggplant and use vegetable broth instead of stock. The same cinnamon-tomato sauce creates a rich, comforting flavor base.

Full recipe: page 54

SPEAKEASY STYLE SEVEN & SEVEN COCKTAIL

Base profile: Vegan, plant-based, gluten-free, and lactose-free.
For lower sugar content: Substitute 7-Up with soda water and a squeeze of fresh lemon and lime.
For non-alcoholic adaptation: Substitute whiskey with a bartender-grade whiskey alternative (Lyre's American Malt or Spiritless Kentucky 74 are options) in equal proportion. To deepen the flavor and replicate the slight oak-caramel sharpness of 1930s Seagram's 7 Crown, add 1–2 drops of real vanilla extract and a small pinch of non-alcoholic aromatic bitters (widely available online).
Distilled whiskey is generally gluten-free; confirm for any flavored variations.
Chef's note: This is a close replica of how the drink would have tasted in the mid-1930s when prohibition ended and Seagrams 7 Crown became legal again.
Full recipe: page 57

KOULOURAKIA

Base profile: Vegetarian, festive cookie with a delicious, crumbly texture.
For gluten-free adaptation: Use 1:1 gluten-free baking flour in place of cake flour, but note that texture will be slightly more crumbly.
For lower-sugar adaptation: Use less powdered sugar (about 2¼ cups) for a less sweet version without affecting structure.
Full recipe: page 59

FAKÈS SOUPA

Base profile: Vegan, Mediterranean, gluten free, high in protein and fiber.
For lower sodium: Use low-sodium vegetable broth and omit added salt.
For paleo adaptation: Replace lentils with chopped cauliflower and
mushrooms for a legume-free version (texture and flavor will differ but stay
hearty and satisfying).
Full recipe: page 61

OVEN-ROASTED CHICKEN LEMONÁTO WITH POTATOES

Base profile: Mediterranean, naturally gluten free and dairy free.
For a vegetarian or vegan version: Substitute thick-cut cauliflower steaks
or whole roasted mushrooms in place of the chicken and halve the cooking
time.
For a lighter option: Remove chicken skin before serving and reduce olive
oil to 2 tablespoons.
For paleo or keto diets: Recipe is already compliant as written, just verify
the seasoning mix contains no added starch or sugar.
Full recipe: page 67

PSOMI ME SOUSAMI (SESAME BREAD)

Base profile: Mediterranean, plant based, and lactose free.
For vegan adaptation: Replace the egg white glaze with a mixture of 1 tablespoon olive oil and 1 teaspoon plant milk or water before sprinkling sesame seeds.
For gluten free adaptation: Substitute a high-protein gluten free bread flour blend (such as one containing psyllium husk or xanthan gum) and increase water slightly as needed for dough elasticity.
For no added sugar diets: Use honey or omit the sweetener entirely. Flavor and texture will remain excellent.
Full recipe: page 69

TIROPITAKIA (CHEESE-FILLED PHYLLO TRIANGLES)

Base profile: Mediterranean, flaky and light crust, cheesy and rich center. Considered celebratory. They make a great appetizer or addition to a party table or tray.
For gluten-free adaptation: Use certified gluten free phyllo dough. Keep the sheets well-oiled to maintain flexibility, as they can dry faster than traditional phyllo.
For lactose-free or vegetarian adaptation: Substitute feta and Romano with lactose-free or plant-based alternatives such as almond ricotta or vegan feta. Cottage cheese can be replaced with silken tofu for texture.
For lower fat variation: Use olive oil instead of butter for brushing and reduce the cheese mixture slightly with more cottage cheese for balance.
Full recipe: page 76

ELIOPITA (ARTISAN GREEK OLIVE BREAD)

Base profile: Mediterranean, savory.

For gluten-free adaptation: Replace with a high-quality 1:1 gluten free bread flour blend, adding 1–2 extra tablespoons of olive oil or xanthan gum for elasticity and moisture. Cover the dough during proofing to prevent cracking.

For low-sodium adaptation: Choose low-sodium Kalamata olives and reduce or omit added salt in the dough.

For paleo or grain-free diets: Substitute flour with almond or cassava flour blends, understanding that the texture will shift from traditional bread to a denser loaf.

... AND SKORDALIÁ (GARLIC DIPPING SAUCE)

Base profile: Mediterranean, vegan, vegetarian, and plant based. Naturally gluten and lactose free.

For paleo variation: Replace potatoes with mashed cauliflower to create a lighter, grain-free version.

For low-sodium diets: Omit added salt and slightly increase vinegar to maintain balance.

For reduced-fat adaptation: Use half the olive oil and replace the rest with a splash of warm water or broth.

Chef's note: Skordaliá is also a versatile base for many dishes. It is popular as a sauce over fish. Thin the skordaliá slightly with a teaspoon of added extra virgin olive oil for a more sauce-like consistency. Spoon over fried cod, then finish in oven for a few extra minutes. That dish, bakaliaros skordaliá, is often served on Greek Independence Day and Palm Sunday.

Full recipes: page 80

PATSTISIO (GREEK LASAGNA-STYLE DISH WITH BÉCHAMEL)

Base profile: Mediterranean, hearty, and celebratory. Feeds a crowd.
If pastisio pasta is not available, bucatini or any other tube pasta can be
used in its place. This dish freezes well and improves in flavor after resting
overnight.
For gluten-free adaptation: Use gluten-free pasta and substitute gluten-free
flour in the béchamel.
For lactose-free adaptation: Replace milk and cheese in the béchamel with
plant-based alternatives and use olive oil instead of butter.
For vegetarian variation: Substitute lentils, mushrooms, or crumbled tofu
for the meat, keeping the same herb and tomato base.
Full recipe: page 88

GÁMOKOULOURA (WEDDING BREAD)

Base profile: Soft, subtly sweet ceremonial bread rich in olive oil and honey.
For vegan or plant-based adaptation: Replace honey with maple or date
syrup and substitute eggs with flaxseed mixture (1 Tbsp ground flax + 3
Tbsp water per egg) or unsweetened applesauce.
For gluten-free version: Use a high-quality gluten-free bread blend with
xanthan gum or psyllium husk for structure. Increase rise time by 15–20
minutes to maintain volume.
For low-fat adaptation: Reduce olive oil by half and replace with
unsweetened applesauce.
For no added salt diets: Omit salt; flavor balance remains intact due to
honey's sweetness and anise's aromatic lift.

Chef's note: A time-honored symbol of unity and blessing at weddings.
Full recipe: page 97

KARIOKES (NO-BAKE CHOCOLATE WALNUT SWEETS)

Base profile: Rich, chocolate-coated walnut confections with the warmth of brandy and cocoa. Traditional celebratory sweets.
For vegan adaptation: Use plant-based butter and confirm dark chocolate is dairy-free.
For non-alcoholic adaptation: Replace brandy with orange juice or non-alcoholic spirit.
For gluten-free version: Substitute cookie crumbs with certified gluten-free graham crackers or cookies.
Full recipe: page 109

KOURABIEDES

Base profile: A rich, buttery almond shortbread rolled in powdered sugar — festive and symbolic, made for holidays and weddings to represent joy and purity.
For vegan adaptation: Substitute plant-based butter for traditional butter and omit egg yolks.
For non-alcoholic adaptation: Replace brandy with orange juice or non-alcoholic spirit.
Full recipe: page 112

PAXIMÁDIA (GREEK BISCOTTI)

Base profile: A crisp, twice-baked Greek cookie similar to biscotti —
aromatic with orange, cinnamon, and clove. Traditionally enjoyed with
coffee or hot chocolate and stored for long keeping.

For vegan adaptation: Use plant-based butter and substitute 4 tablespoons
unsweetened applesauce or 2 flax eggs (2 tbsp ground flaxseed + 6 tbsp
water, rested 5 minutes) for the eggs.

For gluten-free adaptation: Replace flour with a quality 1:1 gluten-free
baking blend, ensuring texture remains light and crumbly.

For nut-free preparation: Omit nuts without replacement; structure and
flavor remain excellent.

Full recipe: page 120

PSARI PLAKI (BAKED BRANZINO WITH TOMATO AND ONION)

Base profile: Mediterranean, full-flavored and comforting. Naturally
gluten-free, dairy-free, and high in omega-3s.

Fish subsitutions: Cod, sea bass.

Vegan adaptation: Substitute thick-cut cauliflower steaks or zucchini slices
for fish. Layer and bake as written to create a plant-based plaki retaining the
same aromatic balance.

For paleo or keto diets: Already compliant; verify wine is naturally low in
residual sugar or substitute with a splash of lemon juice for brightness.

For regional authenticity: In Crete, raisins or capers are sometimes added for contrast; in the Peloponnese, a pinch of cinnamon lends subtle warmth.
Chef's note: This would have traditionally been prepared in a gastra or clay vessel. Penelope used a French oven in the US.
Full recipe: page 126

ROAST LAMB WITH MANESTRA

Base profile: A classic Greek comfort dish featuring oven-roasted lamb cooked in tomato sauce and served with manestra (orzo), a small, rice-shaped pasta that absorbs the pan juices beautifully. The lamb is typically seasoned with garlic, olive oil, salt, pepper, oregano, and sometimes cinnamon or allspice, and slow-roasted until tender before being combined with orzo in the same pan for a rich, cohesive flavor. Important note: if you have vegetarian guests, recall that you used seasoned pan juices in step 4. Simply omitting the lamb itself and serving a bowl of manestra will not result in a vegetarian dish.
Gluten-free adaptation: Replace orzo with short-grain rice or gluten free orzo.
Chef's note: This recipe is naturally lactose-free if served without the optional cheese topping or by using a dairy-free alternative.
Full recipe: page 129

METAXA SIDECAR COCKTAIL

Base profile: Smooth, with refreshing tang. Naturally vegan, gluten free, and lactose free. This cocktail contains no added salt or fat.

For a non-alcoholic adaptation: Substitute Lyre's Apéritif Ambré or Spiritless Kentucky 74 for the Metaxa, and use Lyre's Orange Sec or any high-quality non-alcoholic orange liqueur for the Cointreau. Increase lemon juice slightly to maintain balance; these substitutes are less acidic.

Full recipe: page 134

MEZEDES (SMALL PLATE APPETIZERS)

Base profile: A traditional Greek meze spread is meant to evolve with the season and the company. Many versions are naturally adaptable.

For a vegetarian platter, omit the loukaniko and liver, and substitute roasted peppers, marinated mushrooms, or dolmades.

For vegetarian or vegan adaptation: Remove the cheese and eggs and add hummus, grilled vegetables, or fava spread.

Use gluten free bread or crackers if desired.

For lactose free options, replace kefalotyri with a firm plant-based cheese.

Full recipe: page 135

DOLMADES

Base profile: Mediterranean, gluten-free, protein-rich, naturally free of dairy. Depending on the region, ground pork, turkey, chicken, finely chopped cod, sea bass or shrimp are also commonly used.

For vegetarian or vegan adaptation: Omit meat and eggs. Fill grape leaves with rice, herbs, and olive oil, and serve with a lemon-olive oil drizzle instead of avgolemono.

For paleo adaptation: Replace rice with riced cauliflower or finely chopped vegetables and cook gently to preserve shape.

For low-fat version: Use lean ground meat or omit egg yolks in the sauce.

Chef's note: Commonly served with a variety of dips, such as tzatziki, yogurt with garlic, or lemon-tahini sauce, and are often part of a mezze platter alongside other small dishes like hummus or feta dip. They can be enjoyed warm or cold, and a squeeze of lemon or a drizzle of olive oil are common finishing touches.

Full recipe: page 145

ARNI FRICASSEE (BRAISED LAMB WITH AVGOLEMONO SAUCE)

Base profile: Naturally gluten free and lactose free, this dish's richness comes from the avgolemono emulsion rather than cream.

For vegetarian or vegan adaptation: Replace lamb with artichokes, mushrooms, or cauliflower, and use vegetable stock instead of chicken broth. The avgolemono can be replaced with a velvety lemon–tahini sauce to achieve the same balance of brightness and depth.

Chef's note: A classic comfort food from the Greek countryside.

Deceptively simple, quietly luxurious.
Full recipe: page 159

DIPLES HONEY-FRIED PASTRIES

Base profile: Hand-rolled thin dough strips, fried until crisp, then dipped in honey and sprinkled with crushed walnuts and cinnamon.
Chef's note: A sweet mostly found in the Peloponnesian region. The folding technique (rolling while still hot) was a point of pride among local women. Penelope would have learned to make these before marriage. It's nearly certain they appeared at her wedding or as part of her dowry of cooking lessons. They are served at weddings, baptisms, and major feasts.
Full recipe: page 161

GLOSSARY OF TERMS USED IN THIS BOOK

AGLAIA

(Αγλαΐα) — ah-glah-EE-ah
A Greek female name meaning "splendor" or "beauty." One of the three Graces in Greek mythology.

AGOURA/AGORA

(Αγορά) — ah-gho-RAH
The town square or marketplace, traditionally the social and commercial center of a Greek village. Derived from ancient Greek, where the agora was both a place of trade and public assembly.

ARNE FRICASSEE

(Αρνί Φρικασέ) — ahr-NEE free-kah-SEH
Braised lamb with egg-lemon sauce (avgolemono). A comforting Greek stew from the Peloponnese region.

AVGOLEMONO

(Αυγολέμονο) — ahv-go-LEH-mo-no
Traditional Greek sauce or soup made from egg and lemon juice whisked into broth for a creamy, tangy finish.

BAKALIÁROS

(Μπακαλιάρος) — bah-kah-LEE-ah-ros
Fried or baked codfish, traditionally served with skordaliá (garlic purée) on Greek Independence Day.

BRÍKI

(μπρίκι) — BREE-kee
A small, long-handled pot used for making Greek coffee on the stove.

CHRISTOS ANÉSTI

(Χριστός Ἀνέστη) — khree-STOS ah-NESS-tee
"Christ is Risen." The traditional Greek Easter greeting exchanged during Pascha, answered with *Alithós Anésti* ("Truly, He is Risen"). The response is sometimes mispronounced as *Alithinós*, which also means "true," though the shorter form is the only one strictly correct in this context. Spoken joyfully at midnight on Holy Saturday and throughout the Easter season.

DOLMADES

(Ντολμάδες) — dol-MAH-thes
Stuffed grape leaves filled with rice, herbs, and sometimes minced meat. Served warm or cold with lemon.

DIPLES

(Δίπλες) — THEE-ples
Crispy fried pastry ribbons dipped in honey syrup and sprinkled with walnuts; a celebratory dessert served at weddings and holidays.

ELIOPITA

(Ελιόπιτα) — eh-lee-OH-pee-tah
Savory olive bread baked with herbs and olive oil, typical of rural Greek cooking.

FAKÉS

(Φακές) — fah-KESS
Lentils; a staple legume used in soups and stews such as Fakés Soupa.

FOÚRNO

(Φούρνο) — FOO-rnoh
Literally "oven." In this book, it refers to a neighborhood gathering place named after the remains of a communal brick oven that once stood there.
GAMOKOULOURA

(Γαμοκούλουρα) —gah-moh-KOO-loo-rah
"Wedding bread," elaborately braided and decorated, symbolizing prosperity and unity.

HORIATIKI

(Χωριάτικη) — hoh-ree-AH-tee-kee
Literally "village salad." The authentic Greek salad with tomatoes, cucumber, onion, olives, and feta, without lettuce.

HORIO

(Χωριό) — hoh-RYOH
Village or small town; the heart of traditional Greek life.

KAPAMÁ

(Καπάμα) — kah-pah-MAH
Tomato-cinnamon sauce, traditionally served with braised chicken, and orzo or pasta.

KEFALOTYRI

(Κεφαλοτύρι) — keh-fah-loh-TEE-ree
A hard, salty sheep's milk cheese used for grating or frying (as in saganaki).

KORÓNI

(Κορώνη) — koh-ROH-nee
Historic seaside town in the Peloponnese, known for Venetian architecture and olive oil production. Birthplace of Penelope.

KOÚKLA

(Κούκλα) — KOO-kla
An affectionate Greek term meaning "doll" or "beautiful girl." Commonly used as a term of endearment, especially for children or loved ones, to express warmth and admiration.

KOURABIEDES

(Κουραμπιέδες) — koo-rah-BYEH-thes
Buttery almond shortbread cookies rolled in powdered sugar, symbolizing joy and purity during holidays and weddings.

KALAMÁTA

(Καλαμάτα) — kah-lah-MAH-tah
City in the Peloponnese, famed for its olives and as a regional trade hub.

KYRIOS

(Κύριος) — KEE-ree-os
Formal Greek title of respect meaning "Mister" or "Sir."

KYRIA

(Κυρία) — Kee-REE-ah
Formal Greek title meaning "Mrs." or "Lady."

MANESTRA

(Μανέστρα) — mah-NESS-trah
A comforting dish of orzo pasta baked in tomato sauce, often with lamb or beef.

METAXA

Μεταξά (Metaxá)
A Greek amber spirit invented in 1888 by Spyros Metaxas, made by

blending aged brandy with Muscat wine and secret herbs. Known for its smoothness and honeyed aroma, it became a celebratory drink in Greek homes and tavernas alike.

MEZEDES

(Μεζέδες) — meh-ZEH-thes
Small plates or appetizers served with drinks; the Greek equivalent of tapas.

O AMERIKÁNOS

(Ο Αμερικάνος) — oh ah-meh-ree-KAH-nos
"The American." A term sometimes used by Greeks to affectionately or humorously describe those who have adopted American customs.

ORZO

(κριθαράκι) — KRITH-ah-rah-kee
Rice-shaped pasta often used in soups and casseroles such as manestra.

PASTÍTSIO

(Παστίτσιο) — pah-STEE-tsyo
Layered pasta dish with ground meat and béchamel sauce, sometimes called "Greek lasagna."

PAXIMÁDIA

(Παξιμάδια) — pah-xee-MAH-thyah
Twice-baked Greek biscuits similar to biscotti, often flavored with orange and cinnamon.

PELOPÓNNĒSOS

(Πελοπόννησος) — peh-loh-POH-nee-sos
Peninsula in southern Greece, rich in ancient and modern history.

PENELOPE

(Πηνελόπη) — Pee-neh-LOH-pee
Greek female name meaning "weaver." In Homer's Odyssey, the faithful wife of Odysseus.

PSARI PLAKÍ

(Ψάρι Πλακί) — PSAH-ree plah-KEE
Baked fish, typically branzino or cod, cooked with onions, tomatoes, olive oil, and herbs.

PSOMÍ

(Ψωμί) — psoh-MEE
Bread.

PSOMÍ ME SOUSÁMI

(Ψωμί με Σουσάμι) — psoh-MEE meh soo-SAH-mee
"Village bread" topped with sesame seeds, golden and aromatic. A traditional table bread served daily in Greek homes.

SANDIA

(σαν-ΔΙ-α) — san-DEE-ah
Author's given name. Pronounced like the Spanish word for watermelon, with emphasis on the "í".

SIDERITIS

(Σιδηρίτης) — see-thee-REE-tees
A herbal plant, native to the Greek mountains.

SKORDALIÁ

(Σκορδαλιά) — Garlic purée made with potatoes or bread, blended with olive oil, vinegar, and almonds or walnuts. Served with fried cod (bakaliaros).

STIFADO

(Στιφάδο) — stee-FAH-tho
Traditional slow-cooked stew made with onions and red wine, usually beef or rabbit.

TARÁTSA

(Ταράτσα) — tah-RAH-tsah
Rooftop terrace; common feature in Greek village homes.

THEO

(Θείος) — THEE-ohs
Literally "uncle." Used affectionately for any older male friend or relative.

TIROPITÁKIA

(Τυροπιτάκια) — tee-roh-pee-TAH-kee-ah
Small cheese-filled phyllo pastries made with feta and eggs, often served as appetizers or at celebrations.

TRÁPEZA

(Τράπεζα) — TRAH-peh-za
Literally means "table." In this book, it refers to a weekly gathering of men in a household or café for cards, coffee, and conversation. Also the root of the modern Greek word for "bank," which originally referred to the moneylenders' tables in early marketplaces.

VASILIKÍ

Βασιλική (Vasilikí) — vah-see-lee-KEE
A Greek female name meaning "royal" or "queenly." Mary's mother Belle's given name, reflecting both grace and quiet authority.

YASOU

(Γειά σου) — YAH-soo
Toast meaning "cheers" or "to our health."

YIA-YIA

(Γιαγιά) — yah-YAH
Grandmother; term of endearment and respect for matriarchs in Greek families.

ATTRIBUTIONS

PAGE 15: PASSENGER AND CREW LISTS OF VESSELS ARRIVING AT NEW YORK, NEW YORK, 1897–1957.
MICROFILM PUBLICATION T715, RECORDS OF THE IMMIGRATION AND NATURALIZATION SERVICE, RECORD GROUP 85. NATIONAL ARCHIVES, WASHINGTON, D.C.

PAGE 28: LOUIS HARRISON, IN HIS MILITARY UNIFORM, C. 1912.
REPRODUCED COURTESY OF THE PRIVATE COLLECTION OF LEWIS HARRISON.

PAGE 34: LOUIS AND PENELOPE IN THEIR CANDY STORE IN THE EAST ST. LOUIS, ILLINOIS AREA, C. 1915.
REPRODUCED COURTESY OF THE PRIVATE COLLECTION OF SANDIA HARRISON.

PAGE 48: VASILEFS CONSTANTINOS, BOARDING SCENE, PIRAEUS, GREECE, C. MARCH 1917.
PHOTOGRAPH BY "OPÉRATEUR K," SECTION PHOTOGRAPHIQUE DE L'ARMÉE. MÉDIATHÈQUE DE L'ARCHITECTURE ET DU PATRIMOINE, FRANCE. PUBLIC DOMAIN.

PAGE 49: VASILEFS CONSTANTINOS, "CROISEUR AUXILIAIRE FRANÇAIS DE 1ER RANG – PAR GROSSE MER PRÈS DE X…," C. 1917.
REAL PHOTO POSTCARD. PUBLIC DOMAIN.

PAGE 51: MARIA TSETSOS BEHIND THE LUNCH COUNTER OF THE SHOP SHE OWNED WITH HER HUSBAND THOMAS IN LOS ANGELES. UNDATED, C. 1920.

REPRODUCED COURTESY OF THE PRIVATE COLLECTION OF KATHY CRANE.

PAGE 71: AMSBURY HOT SPRINGS HOTEL, LAKE ELSINORE, CALIFORNIA, POSTMARKED 1939.

REAL PHOTO POSTCARD. PUBLIC DOMAIN.

PAGE 74: MARY AS A YOUNG GIRL, WITH HER FATHER JAMES AND MOTHER BELLE, C. EARLY 1920S.

REPRODUCED COURTESY OF THE PRIVATE COLLECTION OF KATHY CRANE.

PAGE 70: STAMPED PASSPORT PHOTO AND NATURALIZATION RECORDS OF DR. NICKOLAS THOMAS TSETSOS/CHESTER

IMAGES COURTESY OF ANCESTRY.COM.
U.S. PASSPORT APPLICATIONS, 1795–1925 (NATIONAL ARCHIVES AND RECORDS ADMINISTRATION, WASHINGTON, D.C.) AND CALIFORNIA, U.S., FEDERAL NATURALIZATION RECORDS, 1843–1999 (NATIONAL ARCHIVES AND RECORDS ADMINISTRATION, RIVERSIDE, CALIFORNIA).

PAGE 84: "BUD BAR," MARY CHESTER SELLS FLOWERS FOR CHARITY, C. 1942

ORIGINAL PHOTOGRAPH REPRODUCED COURTESY OF THE PRIVATE COLLECTION OF KATHY CRANE.

PAGE 100: THE WEDDING OF DR. AND MRS. NICKOLAS THOMAS CHESTER, APRIL 19, 1942.

SIGNED PHOTOGRAPH BY ANTONIOS ZAMOUZAKIS, HOLLYWOOD.
REPRODUCED COURTESY OF THE PRIVATE COLLECTION OF SANDIA HARRISON.

PAGE 102: NEWSPAPER CLIPPING, "CLOTHES DO MAKE A BARBERSHOP QUARTET," PHOTOGRAPH BY HANSON WILLIAMS. UNDATED; PUBLICATION UNIDENTIFIED.
COURTESY OF THE PRIVATE COLLECTION OF KATHY CRANE.

PAGE 124: GERMAN SOLDIERS LOWERING NAZI FLAG IN ATHENS, GREECE
BY BUNDESARCHIV, BILD 101I-164-0389-23A / THEODOR SCHEERER / CC-BY-SA 3.0, CC BY-SA 3.0 DE, HTTPS://COMMONS. WIKIMEDIA.ORG/W/INDEX.PHP?CURID=5476326

PAGE 125: LOUIS HARRISON HOLDING HIS NAMESAKE, BABY LEWIS HARRISON, HIS SON NICK'S SECOND BORN, 1953.
REPRODUCED COURTESY OF THE PRIVATE COLLECTION OF LEWIS HARRISON.

PAGE 128: JOYOUS ARRIVAL
OAKLAND TRIBUNE (OAKLAND, CALIFORNIA), SATURDAY, AUGUST 18, 1945.

PAGE 129: DR. NICK CHESTER, IN HIS MILITARY UNIFORM, WITH HIS WIFE MARY, IN AN UNDATED PHOTO, C. 1945.
REPRODUCED COURTESY OF THE PRIVATE COLLECTION OF KATHY CRANE.

PAGE 133: THOMAS TSETSOS, IN AN UNDATED PHOTO, C. 1946.
REPRODUCED COURTESY OF THE PRIVATE COLLECTION OF KATHY CRANE.

PAGE 134: LOUIS HARRISON AND HIS WIFE PENELOPE AT THE TAVERN THEY OWNED, IN AN UNDATED PHOTO, C. LATE

1940S
REPRODUCED COURTESY OF THE PRIVATE COLLECTION OF
SANDIA HARRISON.

**PAGE 150: KATHY CRANE AND DEAN HARRISON ON THEIR
WEDDING DAY IN 1966.**
REPRODUCED COURTESY OF THE PRIVATE COLLECTION OF
SANDIA HARRISON.

PAGE 152: PENELOPE HARRISON, 1962
REPRODUCED COURTESY OF THE PRIVATE COLLECTION OF
LEWIS HARRISON.

**PAGE 165: KATHY CRANE, CIRCA 1950, AT HOME WITH HER
PARENTS. NICKOLAS AND MARY CHESTER.**
REPRODUCED COURTESY OF THE PRIVATE COLLECTION OF
KATHY CRANE.

**PAGE 165: SANDIA HARRISON WITH HER PATERNAL
GRANDMOTHER, PENELOPE, CIRCA 1967.**
REPRODUCED COURTESY OF THE PRIVATE COLLECTION OF
SANDIA HARRISON.

COVER ART AND GRAPHICS
SANDIA HARRISON.

RECIPES
REPRODUCED COURTESY OF THE PRIVATE COLLECTIONS OF
KATHY CRANE AND SANDIA HARRISON.

SPECIAL THANKS
TO LEW HARRISON FOR HIS CONTRIBUTIONS.

.